PICTURE THIS
ANIMALS

KINGFISHER
LONDON & NEW YORK

Copyright © Kingfisher 2013
Published in the United States by Kingfisher,
175 Fifth Ave., New York, NY 10010
Kingfisher is an imprint of Macmillan Children's Books, London.

Author: Margaret Hynes
Illustrations: Andy Crisp
Consultant: John Woodward
Designer: Samantha Richiardi
Developed by: Simon Holland

With special thanks to Peter Winfield

Distributed in the U.S. and Canada by Macmillan, 175 Fifth Ave., New York, NY 10010

Library of Congress Cataloging-in-Publication data has been applied for.

ISBN: 978-0-7534-6887-6

Kingfisher books are available for special promotions and premiums.
For details contact: Special Markets Department, Macmillan, 175 Fifth Ave., New York, NY 10010.

For more information, please visit www.kingfisherbooks.com

Printed in China
1 3 5 7 9 8 6 4 2
1TR/0913/WKT/UG/140WF

PICTURE THIS
ANIMALS

picnic area
19 mi. (30km)

KINGFISHER
NEW YORK

Contents

Magnificent measures

This book is bursting with information graphics, or pictures, that illustrate facts and figures relating to animals. Any measurements are shown using the U.S. Customary system, which describes length in feet, volume in pints or gallons, and weight in pounds. If you use meters, liters, and kilograms instead, you are using the metric system (in parentheses). The graphics on these pages compare the two amounts and will help you visualize the units.

Speed

Mph is a unit of speed, expressing the number of miles traveled in one hour. This speedometer shows how mph compares with kilometers per hour (km/h).

Volume

This pitcher holds 35 fluid ounces (35 fl. oz.), or just over 2 pints. This is equal to 1,000 milliliters, or 1 liter.

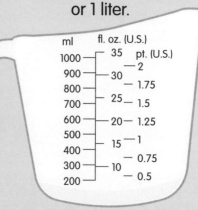

Distance

HIGHWAY 50

Newtown 0.6 mi. (1km)
Townsville 6 mi. (10km)

Length

There are 12 inches (12 in.) in a foot. There are also ten millimeters (10mm) in one centimeter (1cm), 100 centimeters in one meter (1m), and 1,000 meters in one kilometer (1km). This ruler shows centimeters (cm) and inches (in.).

0cm 1 2 3 4 5 6 7 8 9 10 11 12 13

0 in. 1 2 3 4 5

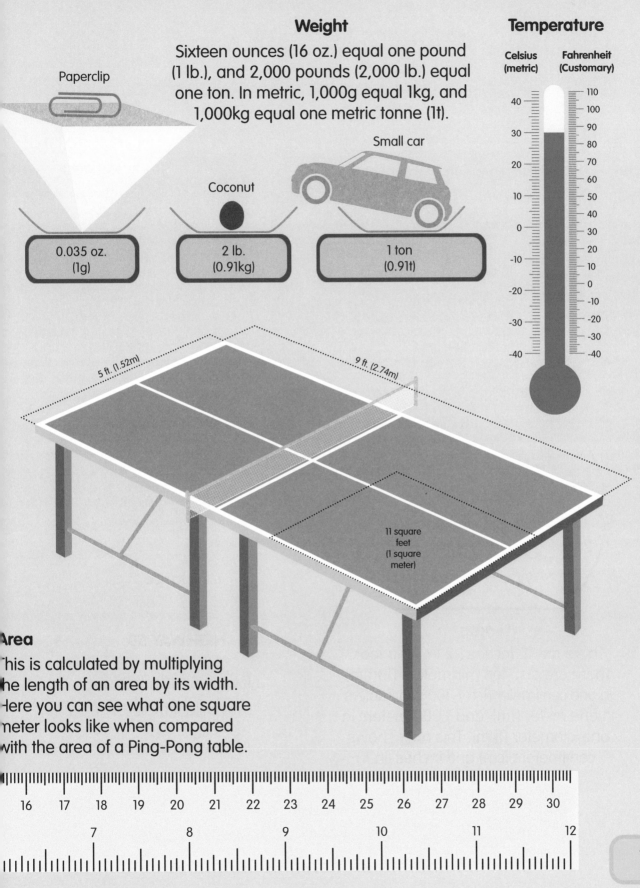

Weight

Sixteen ounces (16 oz.) equal one pound (1 lb.), and 2,000 pounds (2,000 lb.) equal one ton. In metric, 1,000g equal 1kg, and 1,000kg equal one metric tonne (1t).

Paperclip

0.035 oz.
(1g)

Coconut

2 lb.
(0.91kg)

Small car

1 ton
(0.91t)

Temperature

Celsius
(metric)

Fahrenheit
(Customary)

9 ft. (2.74m)

5 ft. (1.52m)

11 square
feet
(1 square
meter)

Area

This is calculated by multiplying the length of an area by its width. Here you can see what one square meter looks like when compared with the area of a Ping-Pong table.

Animal kingdom

When a new animal species is found, it is given a scientific name, usually in Latin, and a formal description that explains how the species differs from other species or how it is related to them. The species are classified, or arranged, into categories based on shared features. All animals belong to the animal kingdom, and all doglike animals are grouped in the dog family.

Animal catalogs

Category	Number of groups in the category
Animal Kingdom	1
Phylum	32
Class	90
Order	493
Family	5,404
Genus	94,240
Species	1,233,500

Classifying *Canis lupus* (gray wolf)

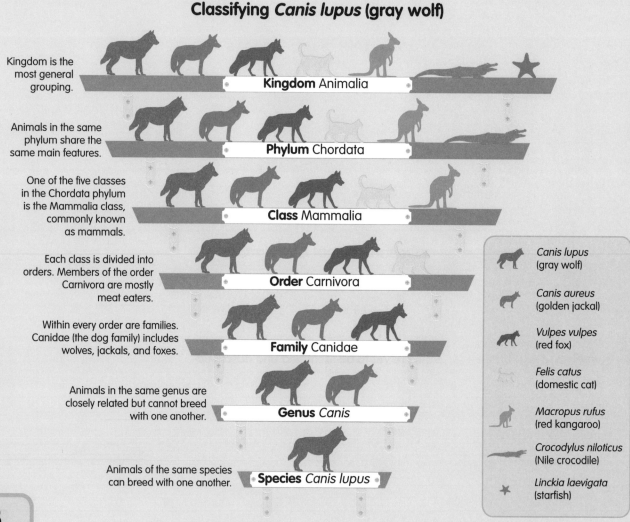

Kingdom is the most general grouping.

Kingdom Animalia

Animals in the same phylum share the same main features.

Phylum Chordata

One of the five classes in the Chordata phylum is the Mammalia class, commonly known as mammals.

Class Mammalia

Each class is divided into orders. Members of the order Carnivora are mostly meat eaters.

Order Carnivora

Within every order are families. Canidae (the dog family) includes wolves, jackals, and foxes.

Family Canidae

Animals in the same genus are closely related but cannot breed with one another.

Genus *Canis*

Animals of the same species can breed with one another.

Species *Canis lupus*

Canis lupus (gray wolf)

Canis aureus (golden jackal)

Vulpes vulpes (red fox)

Felis catus (domestic cat)

Macropus rufus (red kangaroo)

Crocodylus niloticus (Nile crocodile)

Linckia laevigata (starfish)

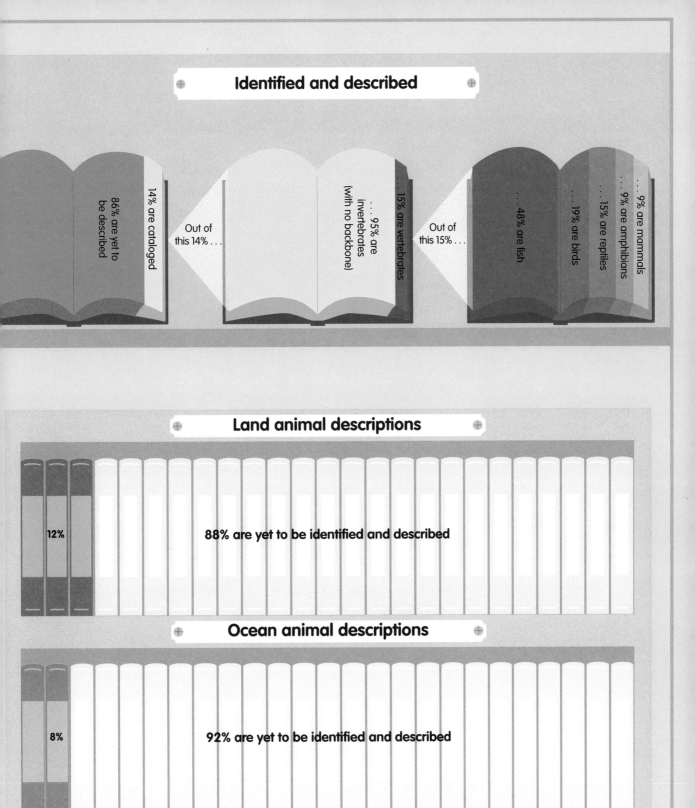

Identified and described

86% are yet to
be described

14% are cataloged

Out of
this 14% . . .

. . . 95% are
invertebrates
(with no backbone)

. . . 15% are vertebrates

Out of
this 15% . . .

. . . 48% are fish

. . . 19% are birds

. . . 15% are reptiles

. . . 9% are amphibians

. . . 9% are mammals

Land animal descriptions

12%

88% are yet to be identified and described

Ocean animal descriptions

8%

92% are yet to be identified and described

Mammals

All mammals are warm-blooded creatures that keep their bodies at a constant temperature by generating their own heat. Mammals also have some fur or hair on their bodies, and they feed their young milk. A few mammals lay eggs, but most mammals give birth to live young. Some of these mammals carry their young in pouches.

Egg-laying mammals

An echidna usually lays one egg. A platypus lays about three.

From Australia and New Guinea

From Australia

Top six mammal groups

Mammal orders (6 of 27)	Number of species
Rodentia (mice, rats, porcupines, beavers, and other gnawing animals)	2,225
Chiroptera (bats)	1,150
Eulipotyphla (shrews, moles, and solenodons)	607
Primates (humans, apes, monkeys, and lemurs)	414
Cetartiodactyla (whales and even-toed hoofed mammals)	330
Carnivora (Dogs, cats, bears, weasels, seals, and their relatives)	285
Known species in the top six orders	5,011
Total number of known mammal species	5,488

Different shapes and sizes

Mammals range in size from the 1.6-inch (40-mm)-long bumblebee bat to the 105-foot (32-m)-long blue whale.

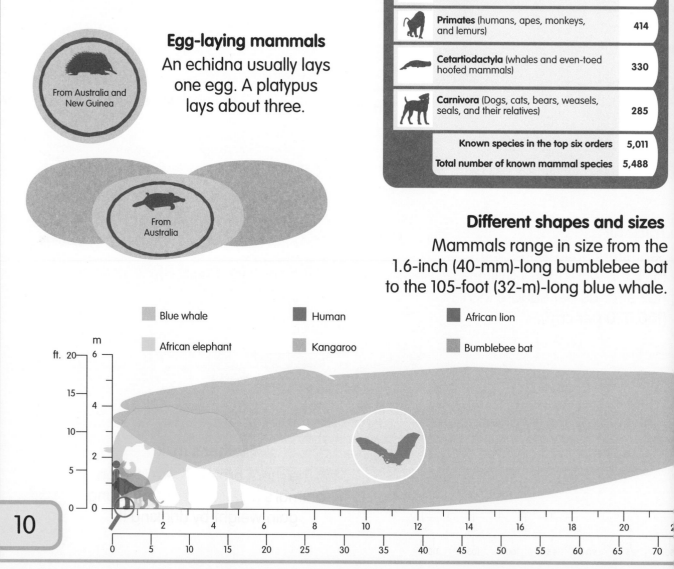

- Blue whale
- African elephant
- Human
- Kangaroo
- African lion
- Bumblebee bat

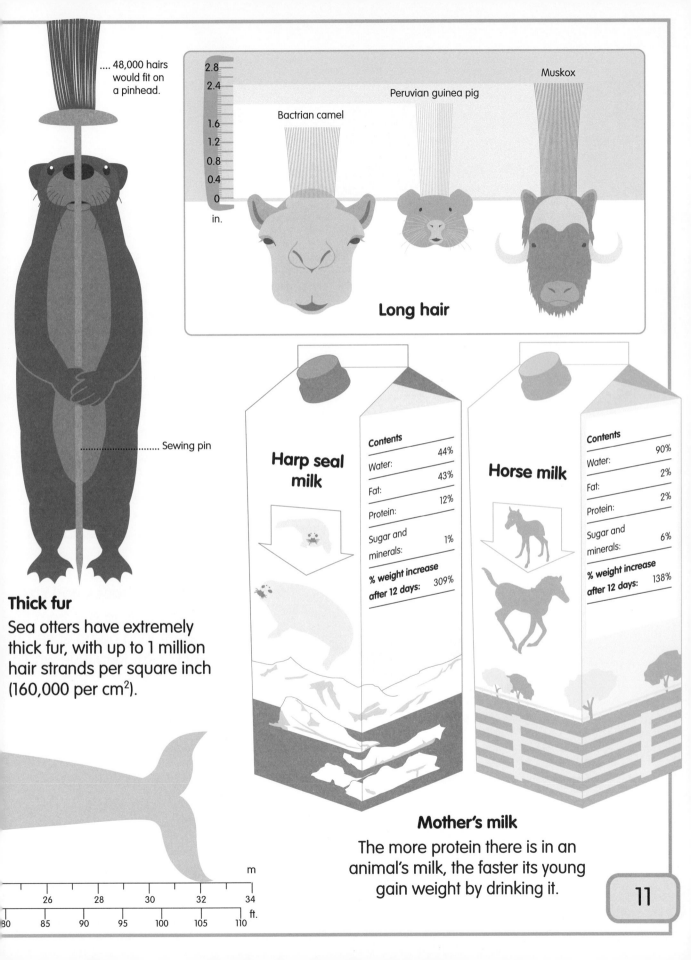

.... 48,000 hairs would fit on a pinhead.

Long hair

2.8
2.4
1.6
1.2
0.8
0.4
0
in.

Bactrian camel

Peruvian guinea pig

Muskox

.... Sewing pin

Thick fur

Sea otters have extremely thick fur, with up to 1 million hair strands per square inch (160,000 per cm^2).

Harp seal milk

Contents	
Water:	44%
Fat:	43%
Protein:	12%
Sugar and minerals:	1%
% weight increase after 12 days:	309%

Horse milk

Contents	
Water:	90%
Fat:	2%
Protein:	2%
Sugar and minerals:	6%
% weight increase after 12 days:	138%

Mother's milk

The more protein there is in an animal's milk, the faster its young gain weight by drinking it.

m

26   28   30   32   34

80   85   90   95   100   105   110   ft.

Mammal lifestyles

In general, small, very active mammals tend to eat a lot of food in relation to their size to fuel their activity, and they produce a lot of waste. Large, less active mammals that graze all day don't need very much sleep. Some mammals hibernate, going into a dormant (inactive) state for long periods of time in the winter, when food is scarce.

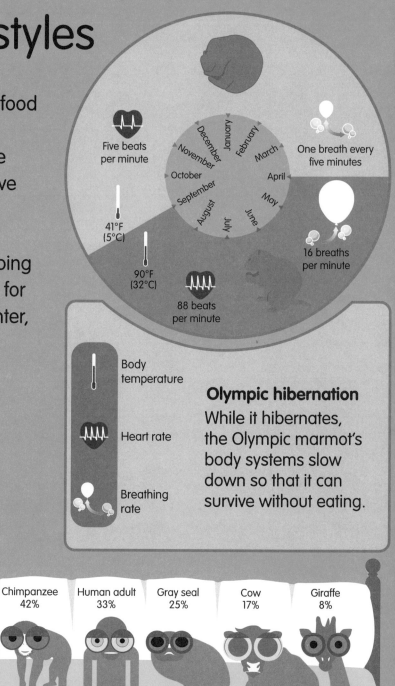

Five beats per minute

41°F (5°C)

90°F (32°C)

88 beats per minute

One breath every five minutes

16 breaths per minute

Body temperature

Heart rate

Breathing rate

Olympic hibernation

While it hibernates, the Olympic marmot's body systems slow down so that it can survive without eating.

| Little brown bat 83% | Koala 80% | Mouse 50% | Chimpanzee 42% | Human adult 33% | Gray seal 25% | Cow 17% | Giraffe 8% |

Sleepy eyes

Some animals spend a large percentage of the day asleep, and some animals barely sleep at all.

Daily food consumption and waste production

■ Volume of food as % of body weight
■ Volume of waste as % of food consumed

Animal size guide

Blue whale
......4%
50%

African elephant
.....6%
50%

Shrew
300%
20%

These animals are shown as if they were the same size.

Gas power
Some animals release enough waste gas to power a 100-watt light bulb.

Human

Pig

Camel

Cow

Annual gas production

0.26 lb. (0.12kg) 3.3 lb. (1.5kg) 101 lb. (46kg) 220 lb. (100kg)

Number of days a light bulb can be powered by the annual supply

0.8 days
9 days
276 days
600 days

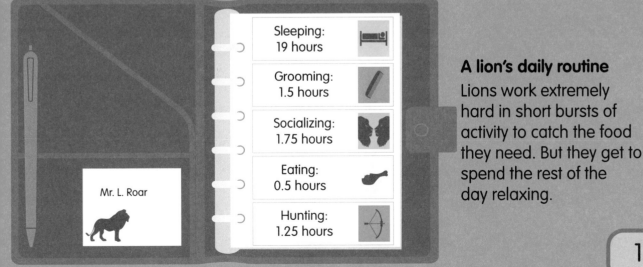

Sleeping: 19 hours

Grooming: 1.5 hours

Socializing: 1.75 hours

Eating: 0.5 hours

Hunting: 1.25 hours

Mr. L. Roar

A lion's daily routine
Lions work extremely hard in short bursts of activity to catch the food they need. But they get to spend the rest of the day relaxing.

13

Bird abilities

Birds are probably best known for their ability to fly. But not all birds are flying aces. Certain species, such as ostrich and penguins, can't fly and have lifestyles that are more suited to the land or water. All birds have feathers and reproduce by laying eggs. These vary in shape, color, and size, depending on the type of bird that lays them.

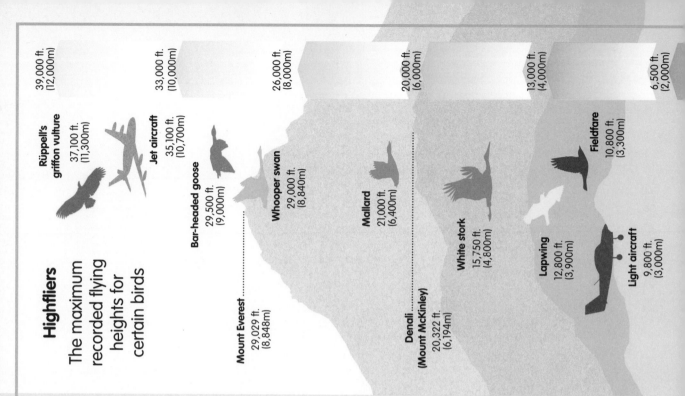

Highfliers

The maximum recorded flying heights for certain birds

Rüppell's griffon vulture 37,100 ft. (11,300m)

Jet aircraft 35,100 ft. (10,700m)

Bar-headed goose 29,500 ft. (9,000m)

Whooper swan 29,000 ft. (8,840m)

Mallard 21,000 ft. (6,400m)

White stork 15,750 ft. (4,800m)

Fieldfare 10,800 ft. (3,300m)

Lapwing 12,800 ft. (3,900m)

Light aircraft 9,800 ft. (3,000m)

Mount Everest 29,029 ft. (8,848m)

Denali (Mount McKinley) 20,322 ft. (6,194m)

39,000 ft. (12,000m)

33,000 ft. (10,000m)

26,000 ft. (8,000m)

20,000 ft. (6,000m)

13,000 ft. (4,000m)

6,500 ft. (2,000m)

Living helicopter

By flapping its wings at a rate of up to 80 beats per second, a hummingbird can hover in midair, just like a helicopter.

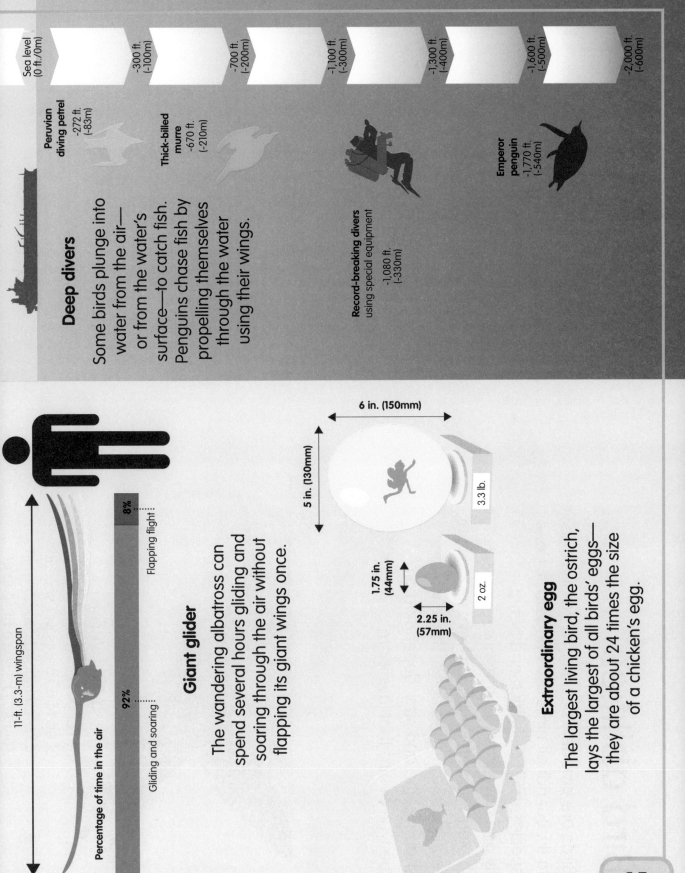

Sea level
(0 ft./0m)

-300 ft.
(-100m)

-700 ft.
(-200m)

-1,100 ft.
(-300m)

-1,300 ft.
(-400m)

-1,600 ft.
(-500m)

-2,000 ft.
(-600m)

Peruvian diving petrel
-272 ft.
(-83m)

Thick-billed murre
-670 ft.
(-210m)

Record-breaking divers
using special equipment
-1,080 ft.
(-330m)

Emperor penguin
-1,770 ft.
(-540m)

Deep divers

Some birds plunge into water from the air—or from the water's surface—to catch fish. Penguins chase fish by propelling themselves through the water using their wings.

11-ft. (3.3-m) wingspan

Percentage of time in the air

92%

8%

Gliding and soaring

Flapping flight

Giant glider

The wandering albatross can spend several hours gliding and soaring through the air without flapping its giant wings once.

6 in. (150mm)

5 in. (130mm)

3.3 lb.

1.75 in. (44mm)

2.25 in. (57mm)

2 oz.

Extraordinary egg

The largest living bird, the ostrich, lays the largest of all birds' eggs—they are about 24 times the size of a chicken's egg.

Reptile groups

All reptiles have scaly skin and bony skeletons with backbones. Most of these creatures lay eggs, but a few give birth to live young. Reptiles are cold-blooded creatures that rely on their surroundings for warmth. They must adjust their activities and behavior to suit the changing temperature of their environment.

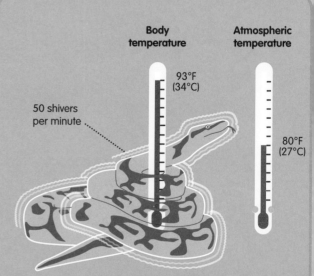

Body temperature

Atmospheric temperature

93°F (34°C)

50 shivers per minute

80°F (27°C)

Shivering snake

To keep her eggs warm, a brooding Australian diamond python coils around them and then shivers to raise her body temperature by up to 13°F (7°C) above the temperature around her.

Powerful bite

The force used by a saltwater crocodile when it bites would feel like the weight of a compact excavator were crushing the area being bitten.

1.9 tons of force

47 in.
(120cm)

Maximum squirt distance

Squirting blood

Regal horned lizards can squirt streams of foul-tasting blood from their eyes to repel attackers.

Reptiles

Order	Number of species
Serpentines (snakes)	3,378
Crocodilia (crocodiles, alligators, caimans, and gharials)	25
Testudines (turtles and tortoises)	327
Sauria (lizards)	5,634
Rhynchocephalia (tuataras)	2
Amphisbaenia (worm lizards)	181
Total number of known species	9,547

Hatch-n-Egg incubator

82°F
(28°C)

86°F
(30°C)

Boy or girl?

Turn the dial to 82°F (28°C), and a male loggerhead turtle will hatch out of the egg. About 86°F (30°C) will produce a female turtle instead.

Amphibians

Most amphibians start life in the water but later change physically so that they can live on the land. They return to the water to mate. Like reptiles, amphibians are cold-blooded animals, so an amphibian's body temperature changes with the changing temperature of its surroundings. These creatures breathe through their skin as well as their lungs.

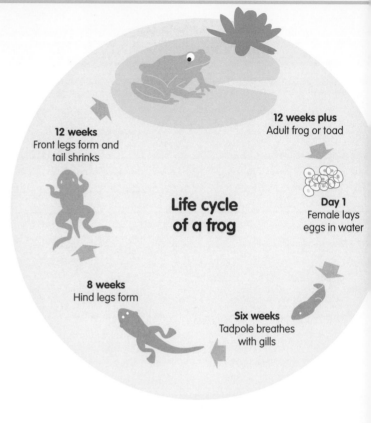

Life cycle of a frog

12 weeks
Front legs form and tail shrinks

12 weeks plus
Adult frog or toad

Day 1
Female lays eggs in water

8 weeks
Hind legs form

Six weeks
Tadpole breathes with gills

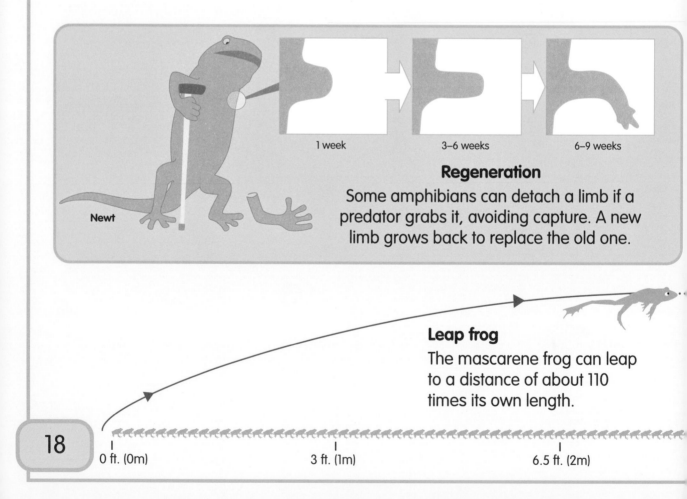

1 week

3–6 weeks

6–9 weeks

Newt

Regeneration
Some amphibians can detach a limb if a predator grabs it, avoiding capture. A new limb grows back to replace the old one.

Leap frog
The mascarene frog can leap to a distance of about 110 times its own length.

0 ft. (0m)   3 ft. (1m)   6.5 ft. (2m)

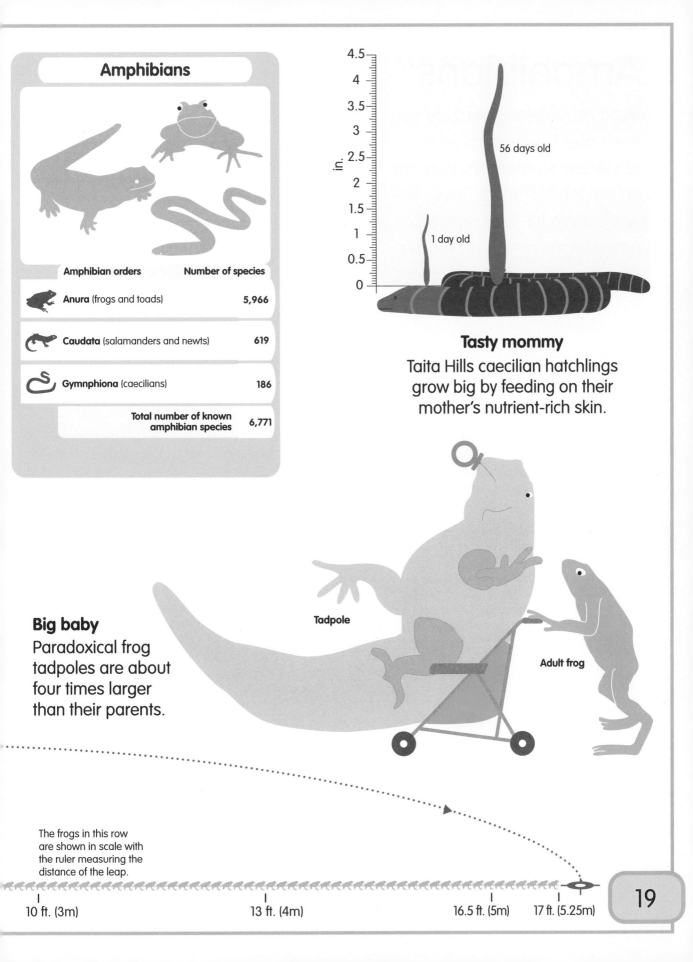

Amphibians

Amphibian orders	Number of species
Anura (frogs and toads)	5,966
Caudata (salamanders and newts)	619
Gymnophiona (caecilians)	186
Total number of known amphibian species	6,771

in.

56 days old

1 day old

Tasty mommy
Taita Hills caecilian hatchlings grow big by feeding on their mother's nutrient-rich skin.

Tadpole

Adult frog

Big baby
Paradoxical frog tadpoles are about four times larger than their parents.

The frogs in this row are shown in scale with the ruler measuring the distance of the leap.

10 ft. (3m)

13 ft. (4m)

16.5 ft. (5m)

17 ft. (5.25m)

19

Fish features

Most species of fish have fins and a tail, have scales all over their body, and are generally streamlined in shape. Fish lay eggs or give birth to live young, and they breathe by absorbing oxygen in the water using their gills. There are three main groups of fish: bony fish, jawless fish, and cartilaginous fish. Instead of bone, a cartilaginous fish's skeleton is made of flexible tissue called cartilage.

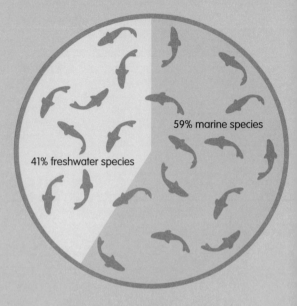

59% marine species

41% freshwater species

Marine vs. freshwater fish

There are more fish species in the ocean than are found in freshwater lakes, rivers, and ponds.

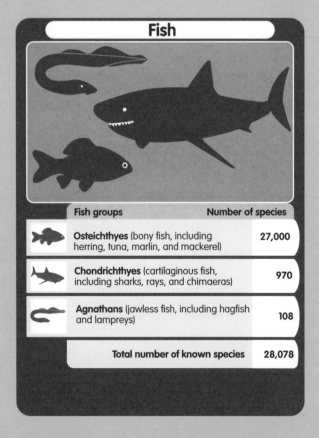

Fish

Fish groups	Number of species
Osteichthyes (bony fish, including herring, tuna, marlin, and mackerel)	27,000
Chondrichthyes (cartilaginous fish, including sharks, rays, and chimaeras)	970
Agnathans (jawless fish, including hagfish and lampreys)	108
Total number of known species	28,078

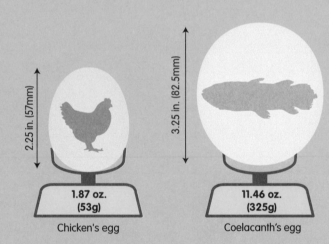

2.25 in. (57mm)

3.25 in. (82.5mm)

1.87 oz. (53g)	11.46 oz. (325g)
Chicken's egg	Coelacanth's egg

Heaviest fish egg

The eggs of a coelacanth fish are unusually large for fish eggs—they weigh almost seven times the weight of a chicken's egg.

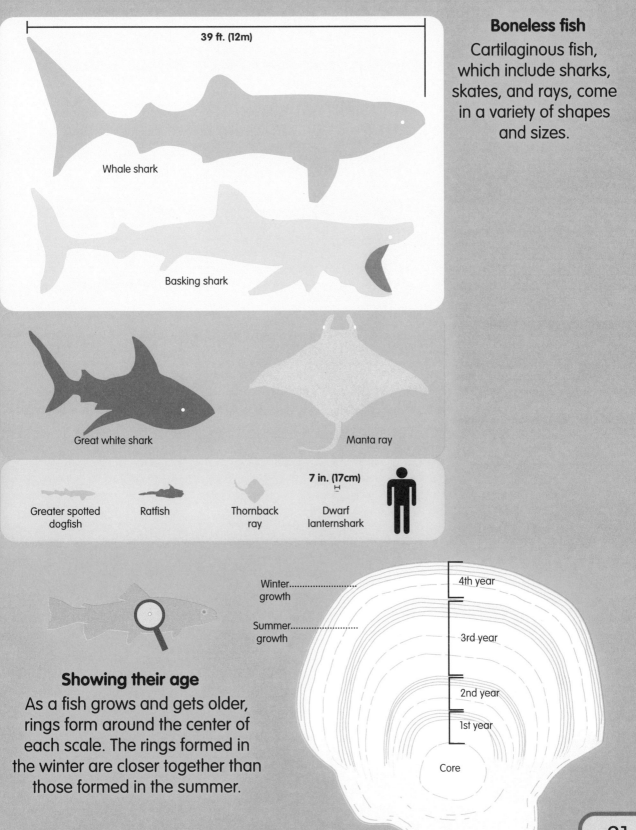

39 ft. (12m)

Whale shark

Basking shark

Great white shark

Manta ray

Greater spotted dogfish

Ratfish

Thornback ray

7 in. (17cm)

Dwarf lanternshark

Boneless fish

Cartilaginous fish, which include sharks, skates, and rays, come in a variety of shapes and sizes.

Winter............................
growth

Summer............................
growth

4th year

3rd year

2nd year

1st year

Core

Showing their age

As a fish grows and gets older, rings form around the center of each scale. The rings formed in the winter are closer together than those formed in the summer.

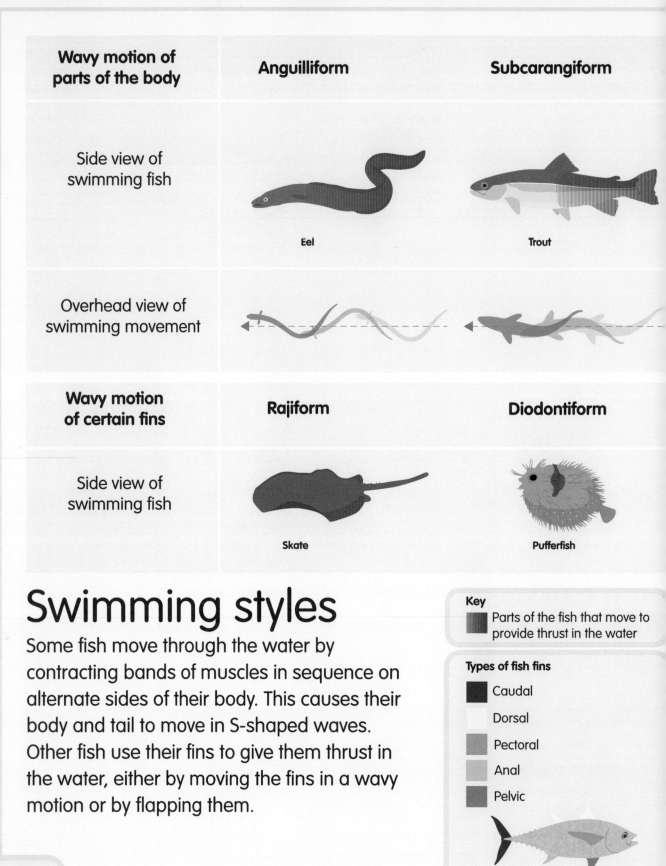

Wavy motion of parts of the body	Anguilliform	Subcarangiform
Side view of swimming fish	Eel	Trout
Overhead view of swimming movement		

Wavy motion of certain fins	Rajiform	Diodontiform
Side view of swimming fish	Skate	Pufferfish

Swimming styles

Some fish move through the water by contracting bands of muscles in sequence on alternate sides of their body. This causes their body and tail to move in S-shaped waves. Other fish use their fins to give them thrust in the water, either by moving the fins in a wavy motion or by flapping them.

Key

Parts of the fish that move to provide thrust in the water

Types of fish fins

Caudal

Dorsal

Pectoral

Anal

Pelvic

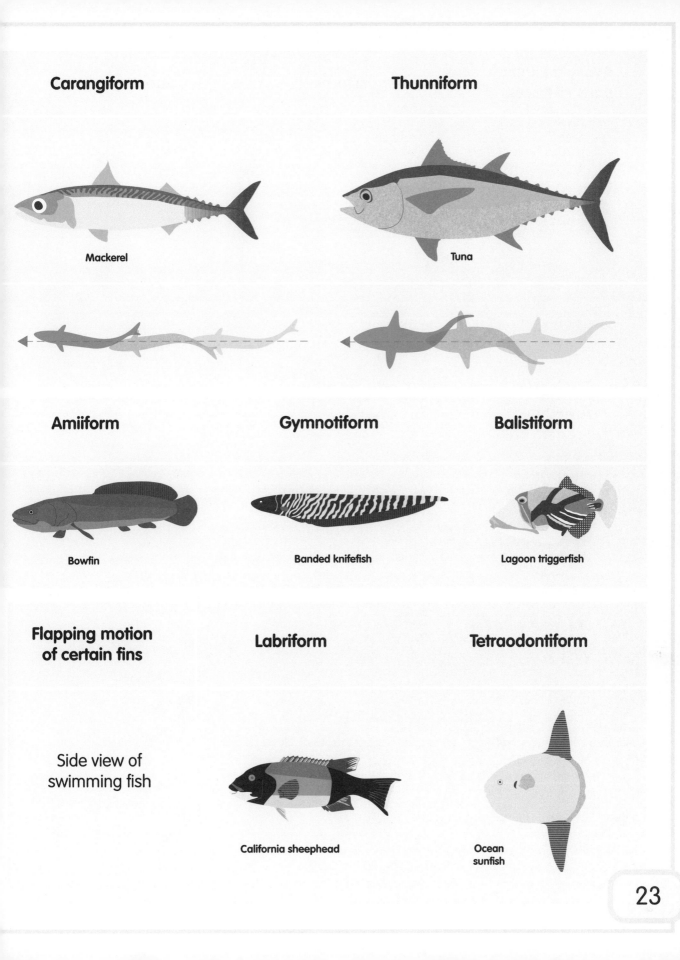

Carangiform

Mackerel

Thunniform

Tuna

Amiiform

Bowfin

Gymnotiform

Banded knifefish

Balistiform

Lagoon triggerfish

Flapping motion of certain fins

Side view of swimming fish

Labriform

California sheephead

Tetraodontiform

Ocean sunfish

23

Deep-sea life

Scientists divide the oceans into layers, including the twilight zone and dark zone. There is just enough light in the twilight zone for animals to hunt by. The creatures here tend to have large eyes to see in the dim light. Many of the animals living in the darkness below 3,000 feet (1,000m) have gaping mouths to make the most of what little food falls down from above. Some of the animals here produce bioluminescent light to lure prey or confuse predators.

650 ft. (200m)

TWILIGHT ZONE

3,000 ft. (1,000m)

DARK ZONE

6,500 ft. (2,000m)

10,000 ft. (3,000m)

Tuna

Jellyfish

Mackerel

Squid

Shark

Ctenophore (comb jelly)

Giant hatchetfish

Crinoid

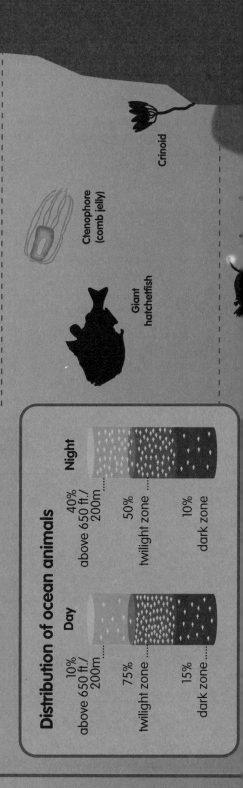

Distribution of ocean animals

Day

10% above 650 ft./ 200m

75% twilight zone

15% dark zone

Night

40% above 650 ft./ 200m

50% twilight zone

10% dark zone

Sponge

13,000 ft.
(4,000m)

Hagfish

Black swallower

16,500 ft.
(5,000m)

Cusk-eel

20,000 ft.
(6,000m)

Spineless creatures

Around 95 percent of all animal species are invertebrates—animals that don't have a backbone. This group includes worms, slugs, snails, and squids, as well as arthropods such as insects, arachnids, and crustaceans. Many invertebrates have outer skeletons, which are molted (shed) by the animals as they grow.

Arthropods and others
There are four times as many species of arthropods as there are other invertebrate species.

World's longest animal
To give you a picture of the giant nemertean's 98-foot (30-m) length, the creature is shown here draped on the Statue of Liberty.

Mirror image
Most invertebrates have a symmetrical body—one half of the body looks exactly the same as the other half.

Which dress-up box belongs to an insect, and which one belongs to an arachnid?

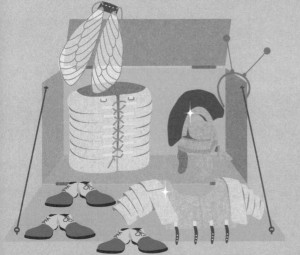

Clues
1) Arachnids usually have eight legs and eight feet. 2) Insects have a head and two body parts.
3) Insects usually have wings. 4) Arachnids usually have eight eyes. 5) Insects usually have antennae.

Molt A

Molt B

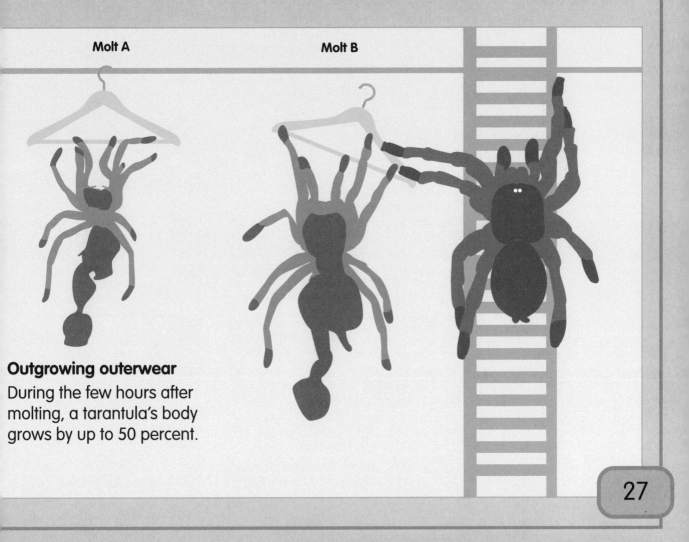

Outgrowing outerwear
During the few hours after molting, a tarantula's body grows by up to 50 percent.

Ingenious invertebrates

Meat-eating invertebrates have specialized tools and skills to help them capture and eat prey. Some invertebrates, such as hookworms, are parasites that actually invade the body of their victim so that they can feed on the nutrient-rich blood inside.

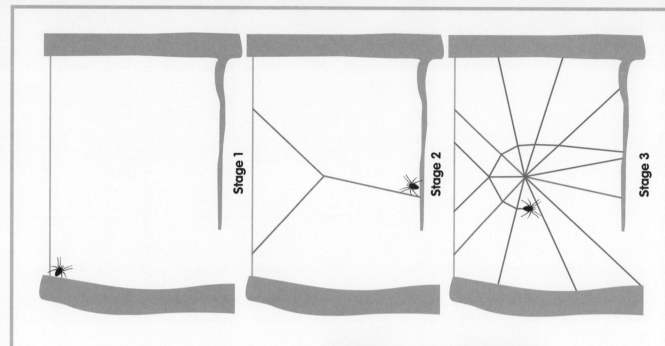

Stage 1

Stage 2

Stage 3

Human blood

The American hookworm and 2-pint (1-L) bottle are in scale.

Power and strength

The claws of the plant- and meat-eating coconut crab can cut through a broom handle and are strong enough to lift an average-size eight-year-old boy.

Weight:
66 lb. (30kg)

Bloodsucker

In its five-year lifetime, the 0.5-inch (12-mm)–long American hookworm consumes almost 2 pints (1L) of its human host's blood.

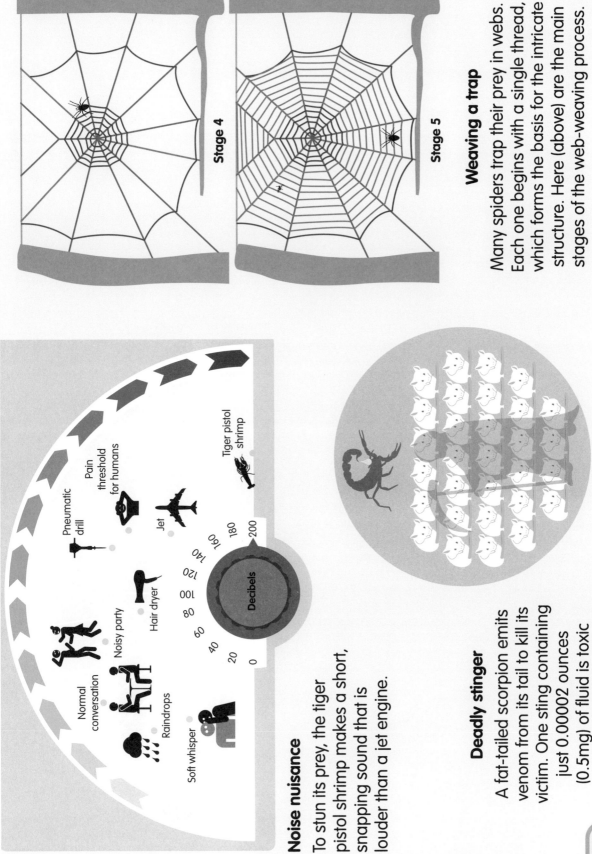

Stage 4

Stage 5

Weaving a trap

Many spiders trap their prey in webs. Each one begins with a single thread, which forms the basis for the intricate structure. Here (above) are the main stages of the web-weaving process.

Noise nuisance

To stun its prey, the tiger pistol shrimp makes a short, snapping sound that is louder than a jet engine.

Soft whisper

Raindrops

Normal conversation

Noisy party

Hair dryer

Pneumatic drill

Pain threshold for humans

Jet

Tiger pistol shrimp

Decibels

0 20 40 60 80 100 120 140 160 180 200

Deadly stinger

A fat-tailed scorpion emits venom from its tail to kill its victim. One sting containing just 0.00002 ounces (0.5mg) of fluid is toxic enough to kill 30 mice.

Minute creatures

There are more animals in your bed than in any zoo in the world. You don't notice them because they are so tiny. There are different types of minute creatures as well—they don't all live in your bed! Any animal between 0.02 and 0.1 inches (0.5 and 3mm) in length is just about visible. Species smaller than this can be seen only under a microscope.

Swells up to 100 times its unfed volume

Hungry sheep tick

Full sheep tick

Not so tiny ticks
Bloodsucking ticks balloon in size while they feed.

Dust mite

Dust dwellers
One tablespoonful, or 0.4 ounces (10g), of house dust contains up to 5,000 microscopic arachnids known as dust mites.

5,000 dust mites

Tablespoon of house dust

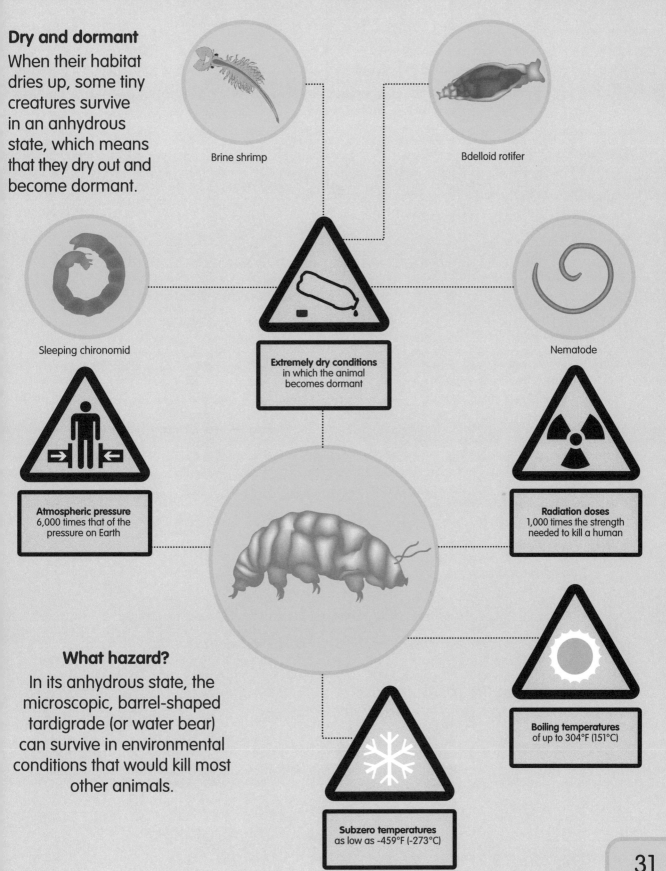

Dry and dormant

When their habitat dries up, some tiny creatures survive in an anhydrous state, which means that they dry out and become dormant.

Brine shrimp

Bdelloid rotifer

Sleeping chironomid

Extremely dry conditions
in which the animal
becomes dormant

Nematode

Atmospheric pressure
6,000 times that of the
pressure on Earth

Radiation doses
1,000 times the strength
needed to kill a human

What hazard?

In its anhydrous state, the microscopic, barrel-shaped tardigrade (or water bear) can survive in environmental conditions that would kill most other animals.

Boiling temperatures
of up to 304°F (151°C)

Subzero temperatures
as low as -459°F (-273°C)

Animal champions

If animals had an Olympic team, they would probably place first in the medal table. The animals on these pages have evolved record-breaking adaptations to help them survive in the wild. Some scientists study these animals so that they can mimic their special features in the design and engineering of materials and machines. Just imagine if there were a robot that could pull more than 1,141 times its own weight like the horned dung beetle can!

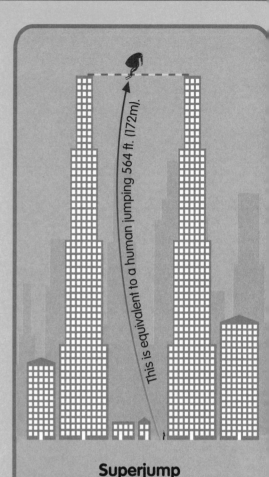

This is equivalent to a human jumping 564 ft. (172m).

Superjump
A flea can jump 12 inches (30cm), which is 100 times its own height.

The 200-m dash

Peregrine falcons can cover 655 feet (200m) in less than half the time it takes the fastest land- and water-based animals.

Peregrine falcon	200 mph (322km/h)
Cheetah	70 mph (112.6km/h)
Sailfish	68 mph (109.4km/h)
Pronghorn antelope	61 mph (98.2km/h)
Ostrich	45 mph (72.4km/h)
Greyhound	40 mph (64.4km/h)
White rhino	53 mph (56.3km/h)
Human man	24 mph (38.6km/h)
Black spiny-tailed iguana	21.5 mph (34.6km/h)

0 ft. (0m)   65 ft. (20m)   130 ft. (40m)   200 ft. (60m)   260 ft. (80m)

Tug of weight
Horned dung beetles can pull the human equivalent of six double-decker buses.

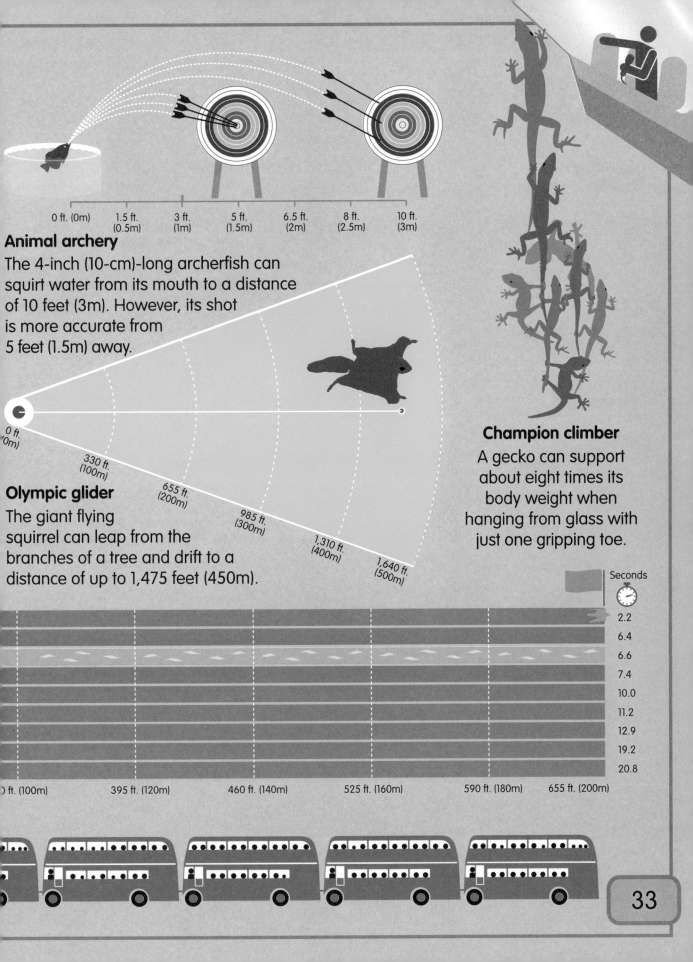

| 0 ft. (0m) | 1.5 ft. (0.5m) | 3 ft. (1m) | 5 ft. (1.5m) | 6.5 ft. (2m) | 8 ft. (2.5m) | 10 ft. (3m) |

Animal archery

The 4-inch (10-cm)-long archerfish can squirt water from its mouth to a distance of 10 feet (3m). However, its shot is more accurate from 5 feet (1.5m) away.

0 ft. (0m)

330 ft. (100m)

655 ft. (200m)

985 ft. (300m)

1,310 ft. (400m)

1,640 ft. (500m)

Olympic glider

The giant flying squirrel can leap from the branches of a tree and drift to a distance of up to 1,475 feet (450m).

Champion climber

A gecko can support about eight times its body weight when hanging from glass with just one gripping toe.

Seconds

2.2
6.4
6.6
7.4
10.0
11.2
12.9
19.2
20.8

| 0 ft. (100m) | 395 ft. (120m) | 460 ft. (140m) | 525 ft. (160m) | 590 ft. (180m) | 655 ft. (200m) |

33

Animal senses

To find food or a mate, or to avoid danger, animals rely on information gathered by their senses. The information is processed by the animal's nervous system, which tells the body how to respond. Many animals have senses that we don't have. For example, sharks can detect the electrical field created by the movement of their prey.

picnic area
19 mi. (30km)

Smell
Sometimes life is a picnic for the grizzly bear—it can detect the smell of food up to 19 miles (30km) away.

Field of vision

Predators' eyes usually allow them to see forward and downward, where they might find prey. Prey tend to have good peripheral and upward vision (sight above and around them) because they can be attacked from above, behind, or the side.

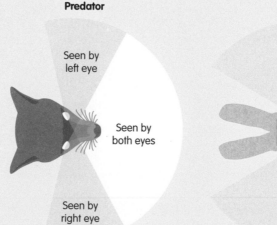

Predator

Seen by left eye

Seen by both eyes

Seen by right eye

Prey

Seen by left eye

Seen by both eyes

Seen by right eye

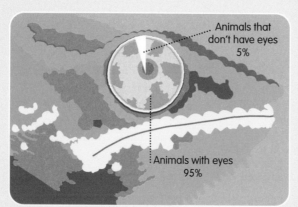

Animals that don't have eyes
5%

Animals with eyes
95%

Eye see you
Eyesight is important for most animals, and almost all animals can see.

Shark senses

Sharks can see in the dark better than cats can, and their sense of smell is 10,000 times better than that of a human. They have excellent hearing, can sense even the slightest differences in pressure, and can detect an animal's electrical field.

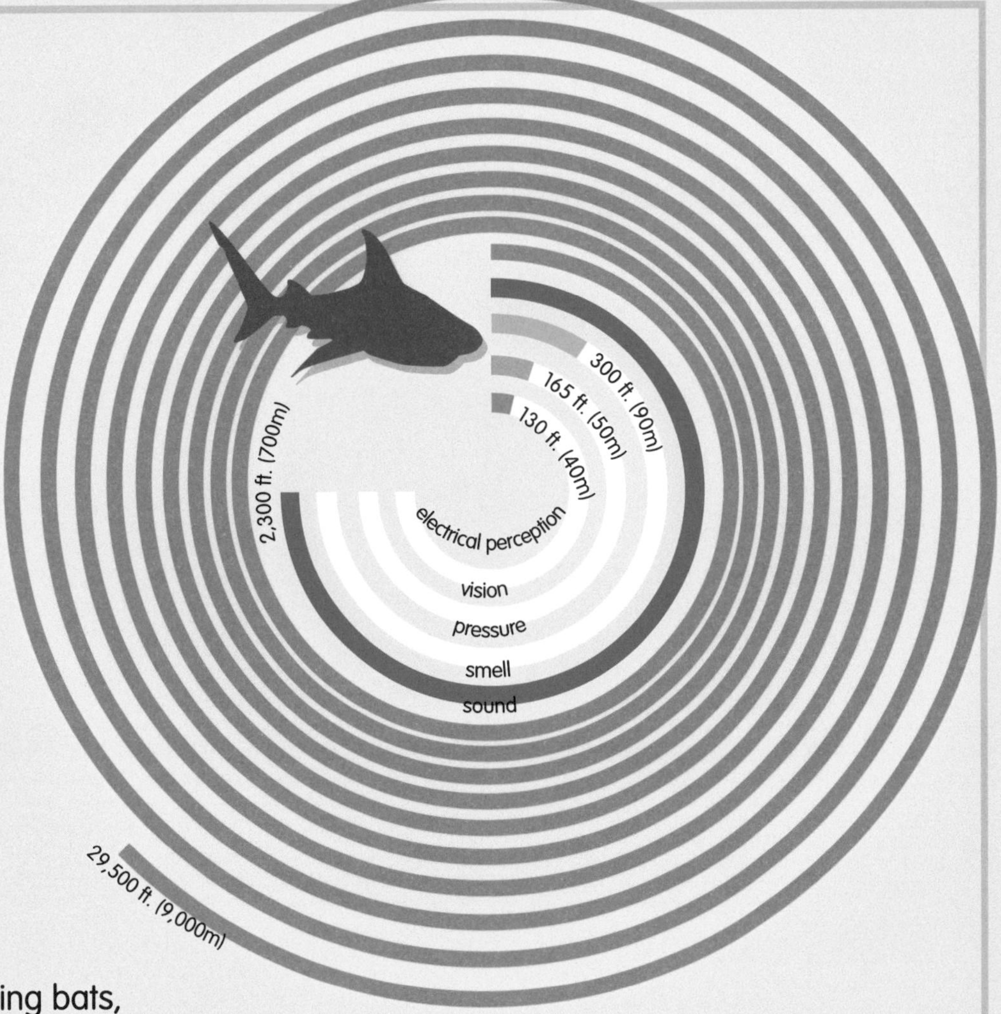

300 ft. (90m)

165 ft. (50m)

130 ft. (40m)

2,300 ft. (700m)

29,500 ft. (9,000m)

electrical perception

vision

pressure

smell

sound

Echolocation

Some animals, including bats, produce sounds and then listen for echoes to find their way in the dark. The delay between the emission of a sound and the arrival of its echo indicates the distance of an object.

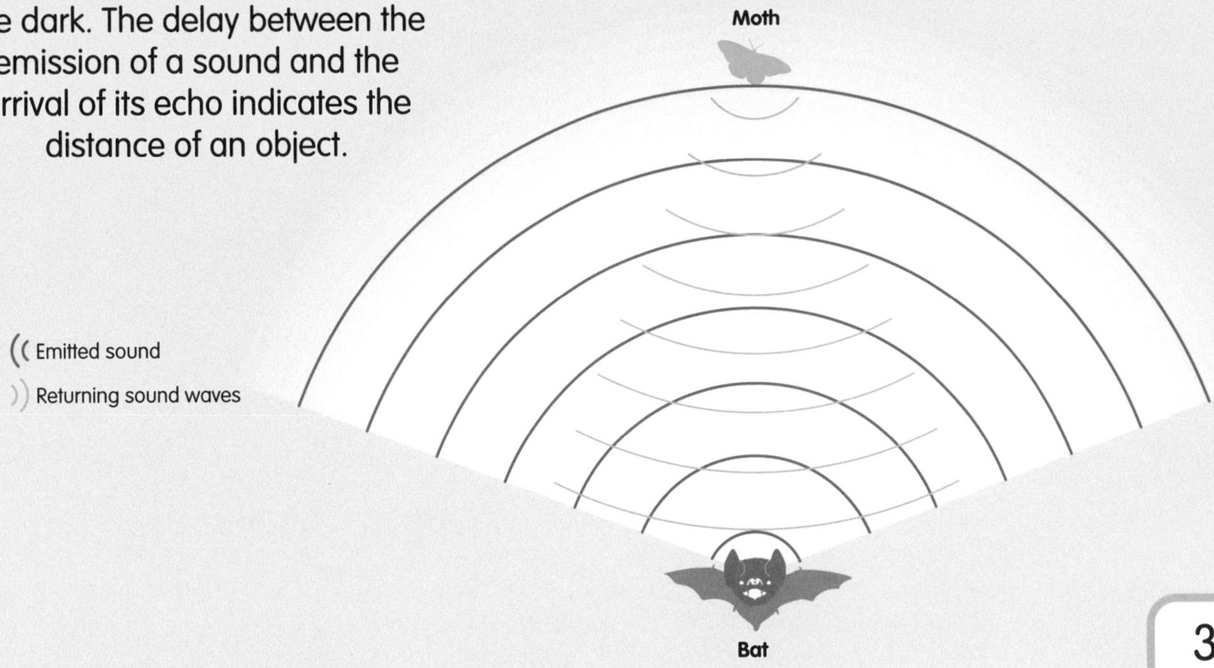

Moth

((Emitted sound

)) Returning sound waves

Bat

35

Communication

Animals might not be able to speak, but they do communicate with one another. To transmit information, they send out signals using sounds, vibrations, displays of color, scent, or even dancing. The signals may be used to attract a mate, protect territory, or warn other animals of danger.

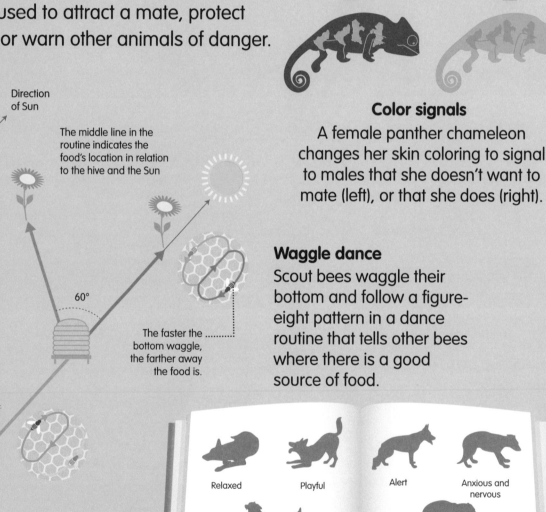

60°

Direction of Sun

The middle line in the routine indicates the food's location in relation to the hive and the Sun

Bottom of hive

60°

The faster the bottom waggle, the farther away the food is.

Color signals
A female panther chameleon changes her skin coloring to signal to males that she doesn't want to mate (left), or that she does (right).

Waggle dance
Scout bees waggle their bottom and follow a figure-eight pattern in a dance routine that tells other bees where there is a good source of food.

Translation guide
Each of these body-language postures (right) explains how the dog is feeling.

Relaxed

Playful

Alert

Anxious and nervous

Aggressive

Frightened

Excited

Calm and neutral

Dominant

Submissive

Communicating LOUDLY!

If all of the animals in the world were the same size, the loudest one would be an insect called the lesser water boatman. Here are the volumes produced by other noisy animals, relative to their size.

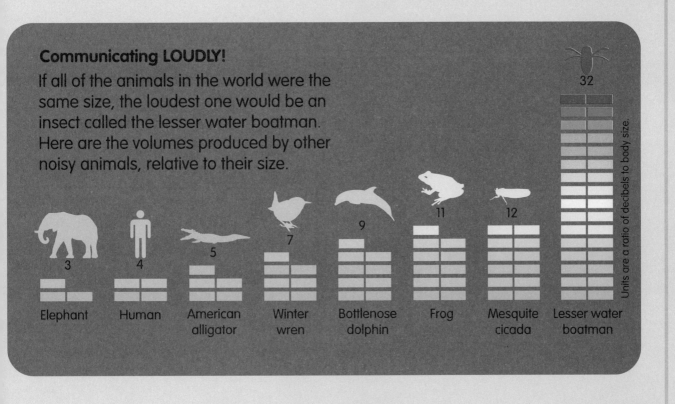

32

3 Elephant
4 Human
5 American alligator
7 Winter wren
9 Bottlenose dolphin
11 Frog
12 Mesquite cicada
Lesser water boatman

Units are a ratio of decibels to body size.

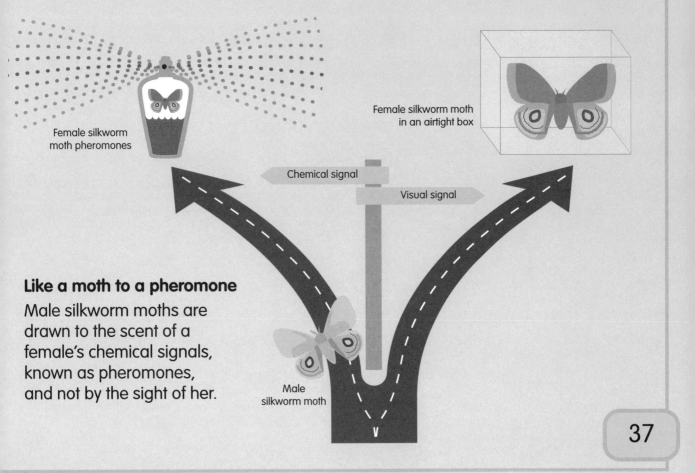

Female silkworm moth pheromones

Female silkworm moth in an airtight box

Chemical signal

Visual signal

Like a moth to a pheromone

Male silkworm moths are drawn to the scent of a female's chemical signals, known as pheromones, and not by the sight of her.

Male silkworm moth

Hunters

Most meat-eating animals are equipped with specialist tools to help them capture and eat their prey. The hunting animals' weapons range from sharp teeth and claws to an ability to poison or shock their victims. There are animals that prefer to hunt alone, and there are those that work together, often taking down prey much larger than themselves.

Hunting party

Some hunters benefit from working in groups of the same species. The size of the hunting party depends on the type of animal in the group.

2 bald eagles

6 chimpanzees

12 bush dogs

Volts

What a shocker!

To stun its prey or keep predators away, an electric eel generates a charge as powerful as five 110-volt electric outlets combined.

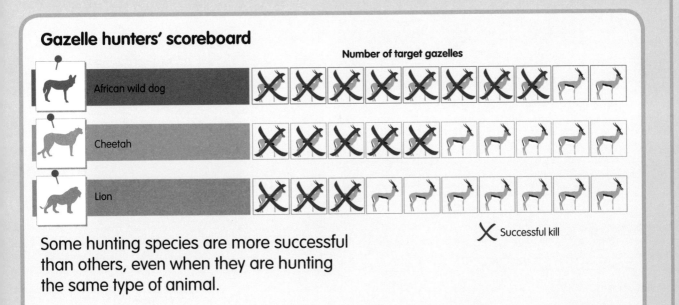

Gazelle hunters' scoreboard

Number of target gazelles

- African wild dog
- Cheetah
- Lion

X Successful kill

Some hunting species are more successful than others, even when they are hunting the same type of animal.

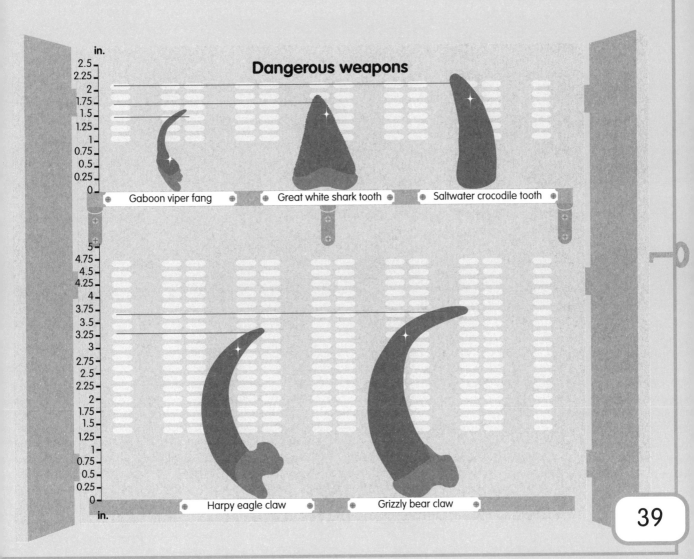

Dangerous weapons

Gaboon viper fang

Great white shark tooth

Saltwater crocodile tooth

Harpy eagle claw

Grizzly bear claw

in.

Animal defenses

To avoid being a predator's next meal, an animal may run away as fast as it can, play dead, or hide. Other animals protect themselves in different ways. Some animals are covered in hard scales or spines that serve as armor, and some repel predators using poisons or stinky chemicals.

Opossum

05:59:00

Playing dead

A threatened opossum can play dead for up to six hours. During this time, the predator is put off by the prospect of eating old meat and so goes off to find a fresh meal elsewhere.

Running scared

Basilisks, a type of lizard, have an extraordinary escape mechanism: they simply drop into the water and run across it. Here is how they do it.

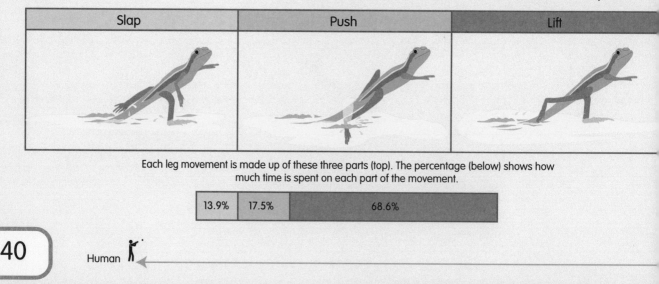

Slap	Push	Lift

Each leg movement is made up of these three parts (top). The percentage (below) shows how much time is spent on each part of the movement.

13.9%	17.5%	68.6%

Human

Stink warning

The average person can detect the stinky smell emitted by a skunk up to 1.6 miles (2.5km) from the source.

1.6 mi. (2.5km) ahead

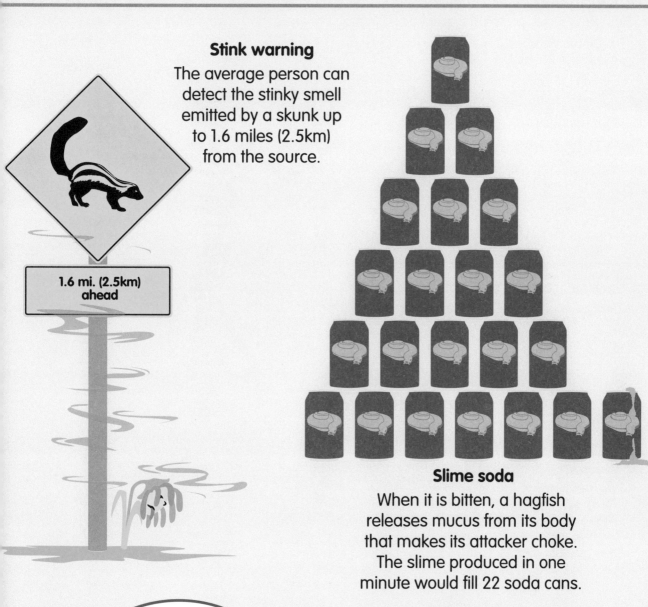

Slime soda

When it is bitten, a hagfish releases mucus from its body that makes its attacker choke. The slime produced in one minute would fill 22 soda cans.

Skipper catapulter

When it feels threatened, the skipper caterpillar shoots poop pellets at its enemy. These can travel up to 5 feet (1.5m) through the air, which is the human equivalent of 240 feet (73m).

This green line is a scaled-down representation of the distance to which the caterpillar could fling its poop if the animal were human-size.

Human-size caterpillar

Criminals

Some animals do things that would be considered crimes in the human world. For example, there are animals that steal food, and there are those that injure or kill other animals, including humans. However, the perpetrators don't commit these "crimes" out of greed, hatred, or spite. They do so out of an instinct to survive.

Theft and vandalism
A locust can eat its own body weight in plant material in one day. Swarms of locusts devour every plant in their path.

Evidence

Suspect: Belcher's sea snake
Description of evidence: 0.0002 ounces (6mg) of venom
Victims: in theory, up to 1,000 human adults if the venom were delivered by some means other than a bite

Possession of deadly venom
The Belcher's sea snake rarely bites. But if it does, the venom that it delivers is toxic enough to kill a person within 30 minutes.

Assault and public disorder
Up to 80 hyenas and one lion have been witnessed fighting over an animal carcass.

Height

6.25 in. (160mm)

4.75 in. (120mm)

Common cuckoo chick

3 in. (80mm)

Adult reed warbler

1.5 in. (40mm)

0 in. (0mm)

Rap sheet

072017

Prints

Name: Common cuckoo
Address: Europe

Charges:
Impersonating a reed warbler for 17 days
Receiving stolen food for 17 days

Identity theft

Female common cuckoos lay their eggs in the nests of other, smaller bird species, which rear the cuckoos as their own—despite the obvious difference in size.

Mosquitoes: 3,000,000	Snakes: 125,000	Scorpions: 2,000	Big cats: 800	Crocodiles: 600

Rogues' gallery: human killers

These shocking statistics reveal the number of people killed each year by the top five human killers.

Courtship

Animals may not send flowers to their mates, but they still do all sorts of things to impress one another. Some of them are pretty wacky, while others are rather romantic. Animals sing, dance, strut, and sometimes even fight to impress a partner. They may even offer food or build a home for them.

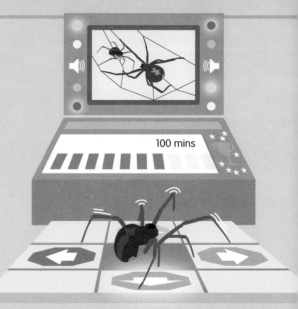

100 mins

Dance and delight . . . or death
A male redback spider performs a 100-minute-long dance to impress a mate. If he stops too soon, the female spider kills him.

Funky gibbons
Every five days, male and female siamang gibbon pairs sing a duet for 15 minutes to strengthen the bond between partners.

0   15 mins

Head-on collision

To win female partners, male American bighorn sheep charge at each other at speed and create spectacular crashes.

50
60
40
70
30
40
80
30
50
90
20
10
60
100
10
70
110
0 mph
0 km/h

Practical prizes

The male in each of these bird species presents the female with a practical gift to prove to her that he would be a useful mating partner.

Fish for a fish

Go nuts for nuts

Nab a nest

Common terns

Northern cardinals

Blue-headed vireos

Growing up

Newborn animals are vulnerable to predators and the elements. Some animal mothers—or sometimes the fathers—take care of their young until they grow big enough to fend for themselves. At a certain point in an animal's life, the creature becomes sexually mature and is able to produce its own young.

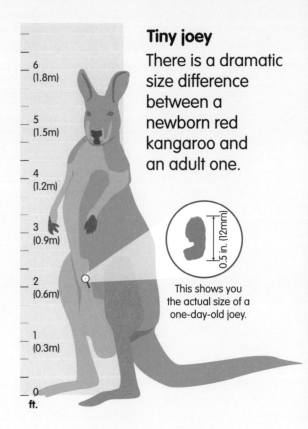

Tiny joey

There is a dramatic size difference between a newborn red kangaroo and an adult one.

0.5 in. (12mm)

This shows you the actual size of a one-day-old joey.

6 (1.8m)
5 (1.5m)
4 (1.2m)
3 (0.9m)
2 (0.6m)
1 (0.3m)
0 ft.

Pregnancy period

The average size of an animal species can determine its gestation period (pregnancy). In general, larger animals tend to have longer pregnancies.

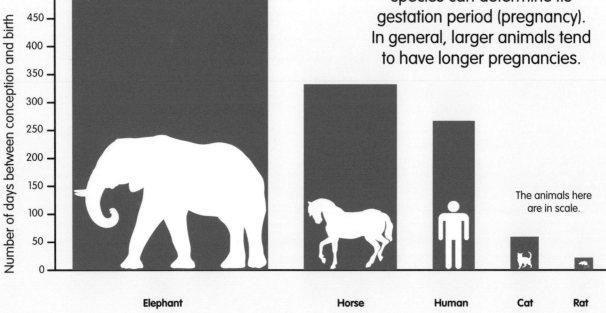

Number of days between conception and birth

650
600
550
500
450
400
350
300
250
200
150
100
50
0

Elephant   Horse   Human   Cat   Rat

The animals here are in scale.

At what point in their lives do animals become sexually mature?

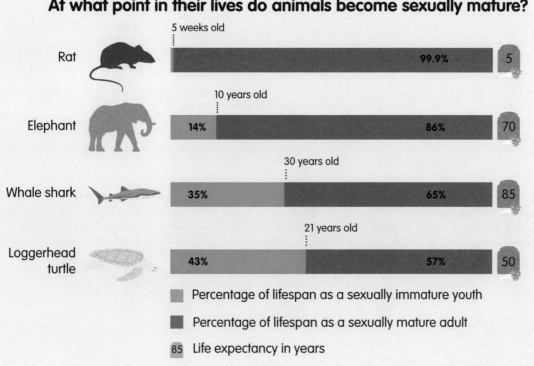

Rat
5 weeks old
99.9%
5

Elephant
10 years old
14%
86%
70

Whale shark
30 years old
35%
65%
85

Loggerhead turtle
21 years old
43%
57%
50

- Percentage of lifespan as a sexually immature youth
- Percentage of lifespan as a sexually mature adult
- 85 Life expectancy in years

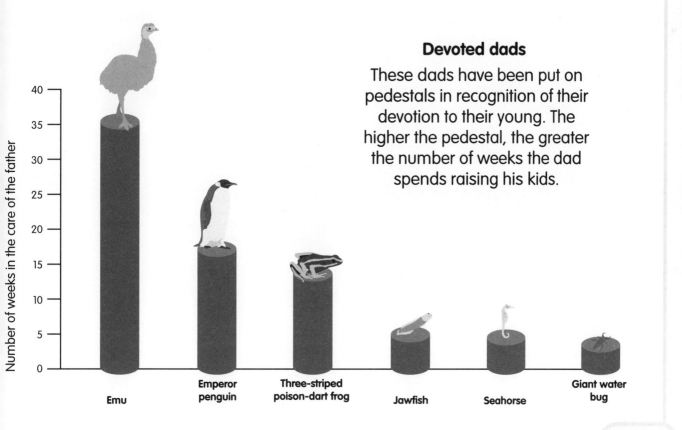

Devoted dads

These dads have been put on pedestals in recognition of their devotion to their young. The higher the pedestal, the greater the number of weeks the dad spends raising his kids.

Number of weeks in the care of the father

40
35
30
25
20
15
10
5
0

Emu
Emperor penguin
Three-striped poison-dart frog
Jawfish
Seahorse
Giant water bug

47

Life expectancy

A Galápagos tortoise born on the same day as a human could live to see that person's great-great-great-great-grandchild. One of the reasons why the reptile lives so long is because it burns energy slowly. As a general rule, highly active animals that burn energy quickly, such as those at the top of this chart, tend to have shorter lifespans.

Expected lifespan

0 years

Bee

Mosquitofish

House mouse

Anole

Newt

Hummingbird

Toucan

Gerbil

5

Kangaroo

Rabbit

Domestic pigeon

Chipmunk

Civet

Sea lion

Leopard

Wolf

Bullfrog

Chicken

10

15

Beaver

Bottlenose dolphin

Dog

20

Tiger

Bat

Cat

Tiger salamander

Conger eel

Cobra

Bison

Tapir

25

30

Horse

Rhinoceros

Chimpanzee

Cockatiel

Grizzly bear

Canada goose

Deer

Lion

Toad

35

40

45

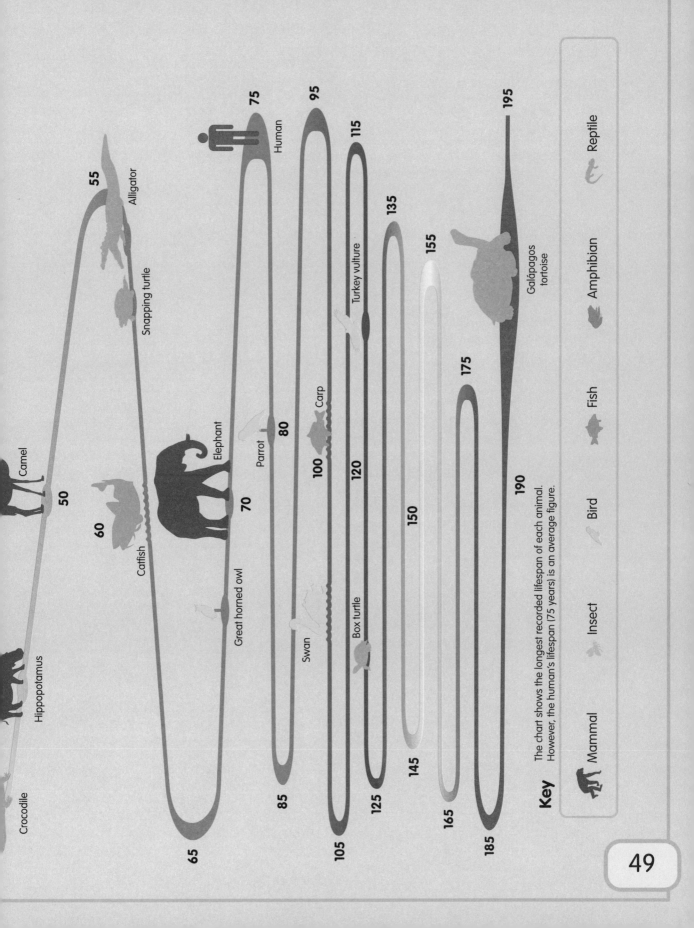

Crocodile

Hippopotamus

Camel

Alligator

Snapping turtle

55

50

Catfish

60

Elephant

Great horned owl

Human

75

70

65

Parrot

80

Swan

85

Carp

95

100

Box turtle

Turkey vulture

115

120

105

125

135

150

145

155

175

165

Galápagos tortoise

195

190

185

Key The chart shows the longest recorded lifespan of each animal. However, the human's lifespan (75 years) is an average figure.

Mammal   Insect   Bird   Fish   Amphibian   Reptile

49

Animal homes

Animals make homes for a variety of reasons. They may need a place in which they can shelter from the elements or take refuge from predators. Some animals make homes in which to protect their young until they are able to fend for themselves. There are animals that spend a lot of time and effort building their homes, while others simply make use of natural features such as caves or holes in trees.

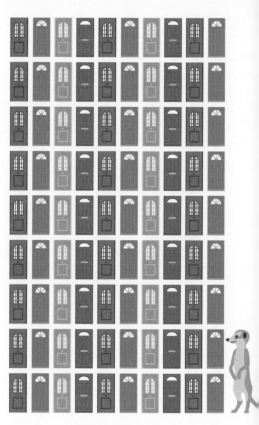

Escape routes
The burrows of meerkats have up to 90 different entrances into which the animals can scurry if a predator comes close

113°F
45°C

149°F
65°C

Keeping cool
The tops of flamingo nests in eastern Africa are cooled by the breeze and can be up to 36°F (20°C) colder than the surrounding ground.

Stone by stone

Horned coots build their mound nests in lakes using more than 3,000 stones. The stones are gathered one at a time by a mating pair.

Home delivery
1.5 tons

Termite tower

If worker Macrotermes termites were human-size, the nests they build would be up to 1 mile (1.6km) tall. The tallest human-built structure in the world is only half this height.

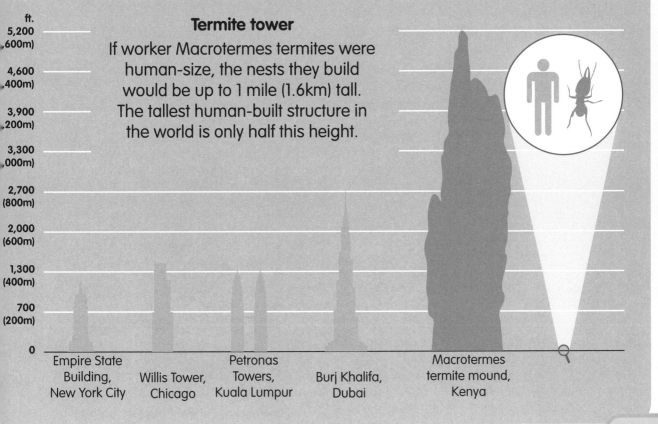

ft.	
5,200 (1,600m)	
4,600 (1,400m)	
3,900 (1,200m)	
3,300 (1,000m)	
2,700 (800m)	
2,000 (600m)	
1,300 (400m)	
700 (200m)	
0	

Empire State Building, New York City

Willis Tower, Chicago

Petronas Towers, Kuala Lumpur

Burj Khalifa, Dubai

Macrotermes termite mound, Kenya

Migrating animals

Animals across the globe fly, swim, walk, or drift in their effort to find food, a more pleasant climate, or places to breed. These needs lead certain animals into difficult and often dangerous treks, some of which span thousands of miles. Some animals migrate each year between their summer and winter homes.

Zoom in to the plains of eastern Africa to see the migration routes followed by herds of wildebeests.

Animal migration routes

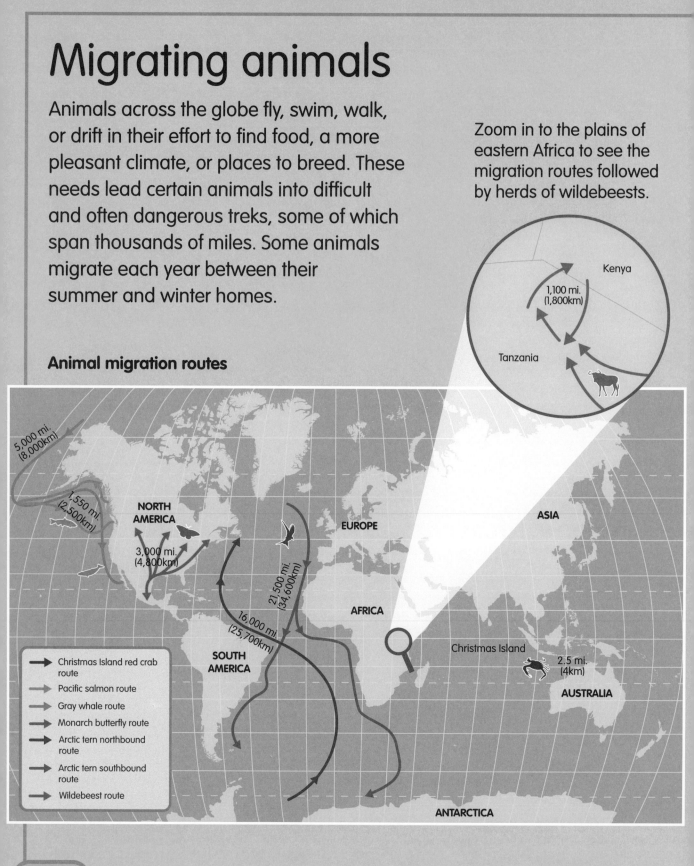

Kenya

1,100 mi.
(1,800km)

Tanzania

5,000 mi.
(8,000km)

1,550 mi.
(2,500km)

NORTH
AMERICA

3,000 mi.
(4,800km)

EUROPE

ASIA

21,500 mi.
(34,600km)

AFRICA

16,000 mi.
(25,700km)

SOUTH
AMERICA

Christmas Island

2.5 mi.
(4km)

AUSTRALIA

ANTARCTICA

Christmas Island red crab route

Pacific salmon route

Gray whale route

Monarch butterfly route

Arctic tern northbound route

Arctic tern southbound route

Wildebeest route

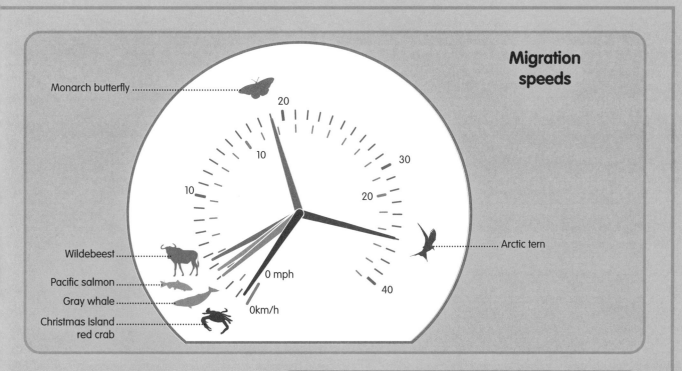

Migration speeds

- Monarch butterfly
- Wildebeest
- Pacific salmon
- Gray whale
- Christmas Island red crab
- Arctic tern

20
10
30
10
20
0 mph
40
0km/h

Out-of-this-world distance

An arctic tern travels more than 1.2 million miles (2 million km) in its lifetime. This is the equivalent of three round trips to the Moon.

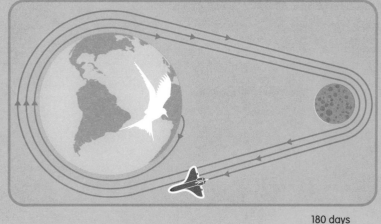

Ready for their annual trip

The number of days our featured animals spend traveling each year are represented here by suitcases and carry-on luggage.

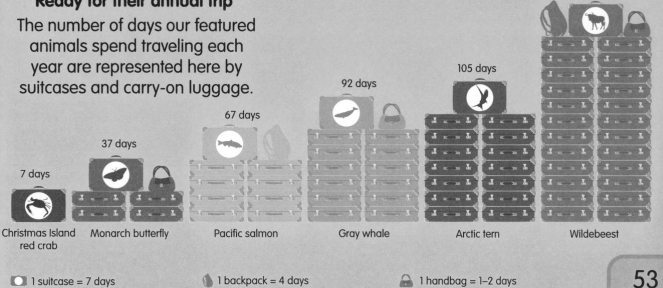

180 days

105 days

92 days

67 days

37 days

7 days

Christmas Island red crab

Monarch butterfly

Pacific salmon

Gray whale

Arctic tern

Wildebeest

1 suitcase = 7 days   1 backpack = 4 days   1 handbag = 1–2 days

Adaptations

All animals are adapted to survive in the habitats in which they live. Their adaptations are physical, behavioral, or both. Over many generations, animal species gradually change and develop in response to their environment, in a process called evolution. The species that we see today evolved from other animals that lived millions of years ago.

Natural antifreeze
The Siberian salamander can survive in temperatures as low as -49°F (-45°C), or even being frozen, by replacing water in its body with an antifreeze chemical.

Animals in cold and rocky high altitudes

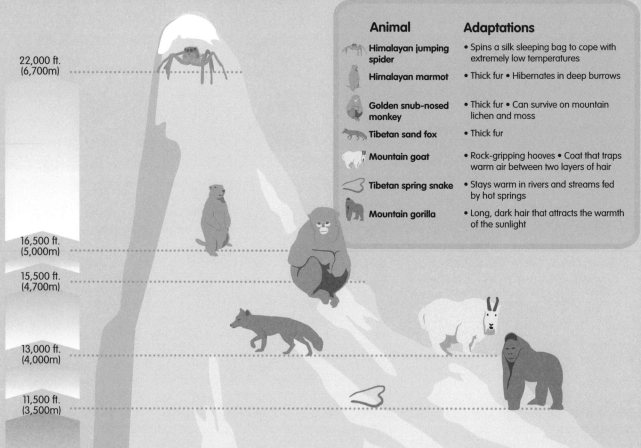

Animal	Adaptations
Himalayan jumping spider	• Spins a silk sleeping bag to cope with extremely low temperatures
Himalayan marmot	• Thick fur • Hibernates in deep burrows
Golden snub-nosed monkey	• Thick fur • Can survive on mountain lichen and moss
Tibetan sand fox	• Thick fur
Mountain goat	• Rock-gripping hooves • Coat that traps warm air between two layers of hair
Tibetan spring snake	• Stays warm in rivers and streams fed by hot springs
Mountain gorilla	• Long, dark hair that attracts the warmth of the sunlight

22,000 ft. (6,700m)

16,500 ft. (5,000m)

15,500 ft. (4,700m)

13,000 ft. (4,000m)

11,500 ft. (3,500m)

Heat resistant

Before it goes out in the sun, the Saharan silver ant produces a protein that keeps its cells working in high temperatures.

Temperatures to hit 127°F (53°C) today

When did today's animal groups first appear?

500	400	300	200	100	0 million years ago

Invertebrates
- Flatworms
- Coelenterates
- Mollusks
- Brachiopods
- Annelids
- Insects
- Crustaceans
- Millipedes
- Arachnids
- Starfish and sea urchins

Fish
- Sea squirts
- Jawless fish
- Sharks
- Ray-finned fish
- Lungfish

Amphibians
- Amphibians

Reptiles
- Turtles
- Crocodiles and alligators
- Tuataras
- Lizards and snakes

Birds
- Birds

Mammals
- Monotremes
- Marsupials
- Other mammals

Conservation

In the past 500 years, human activities have caused many animal species to become extinct (die out). Today, there is a long list of species that are under threat of extinction. Efforts are being made to protect them. This is done by controlling hunting, setting up nature reserves, and by reducing pollution or the destruction of habitats.

Under threat
This diagram shows the percentage of species in certain animal groups that are listed as "endangered."

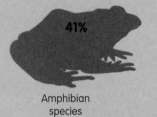
41%
Amphibian species

25%
Mammal species

13%
Bird species

5%
Reptile species

4%
Fish species

A selection of extinct species

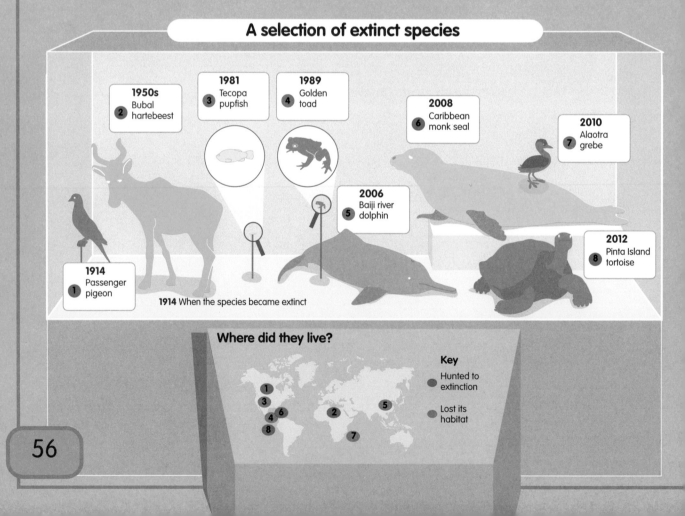

1950s
2 Bubal hartebeest

1981
3 Tecopa pupfish

1989
4 Golden toad

2008
6 Caribbean monk seal

2010
7 Alaotra grebe

2006
5 Baiji river dolphin

2012
8 Pinta Island tortoise

1914
1 Passenger pigeon

1914 When the species became extinct

Where did they live?

Key
Hunted to extinction

Lost its habitat

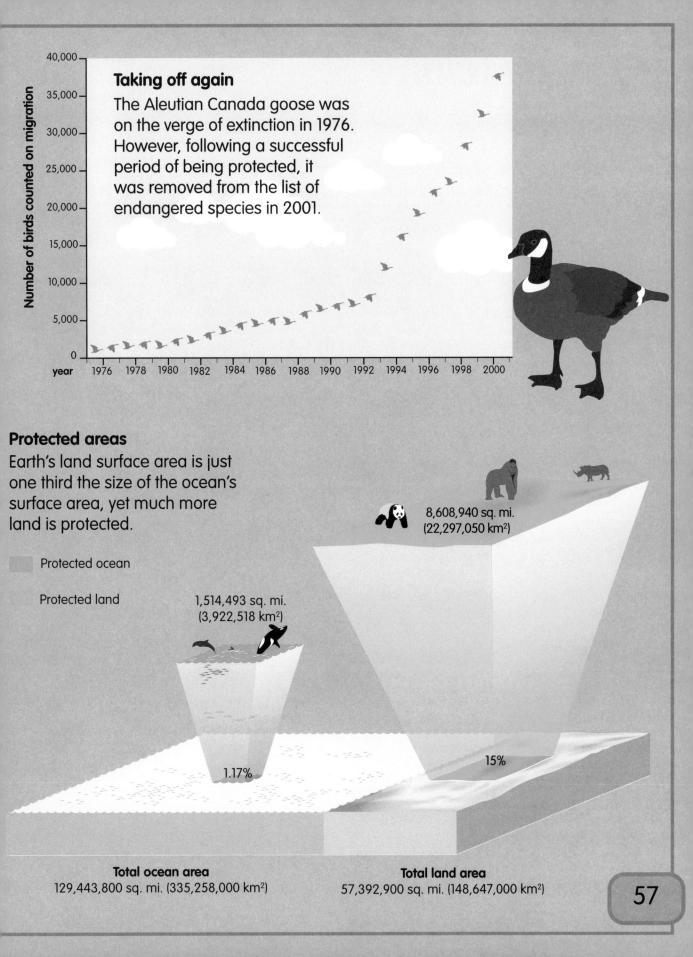

Taking off again

The Aleutian Canada goose was on the verge of extinction in 1976. However, following a successful period of being protected, it was removed from the list of endangered species in 2001.

Number of birds counted on migration (y-axis): 0, 5,000, 10,000, 15,000, 20,000, 25,000, 30,000, 35,000, 40,000

year (x-axis): 1976, 1978, 1980, 1982, 1984, 1986, 1988, 1990, 1992, 1994, 1996, 1998, 2000

Protected areas

Earth's land surface area is just one third the size of the ocean's surface area, yet much more land is protected.

Protected ocean

Protected land

8,608,940 sq. mi.
(22,297,050 km²)

1,514,493 sq. mi.
(3,922,518 km²)

1.17%

15%

Total ocean area
129,443,800 sq. mi. (335,258,000 km²)

Total land area
57,392,900 sq. mi. (148,647,000 km²)

57

Useful charts

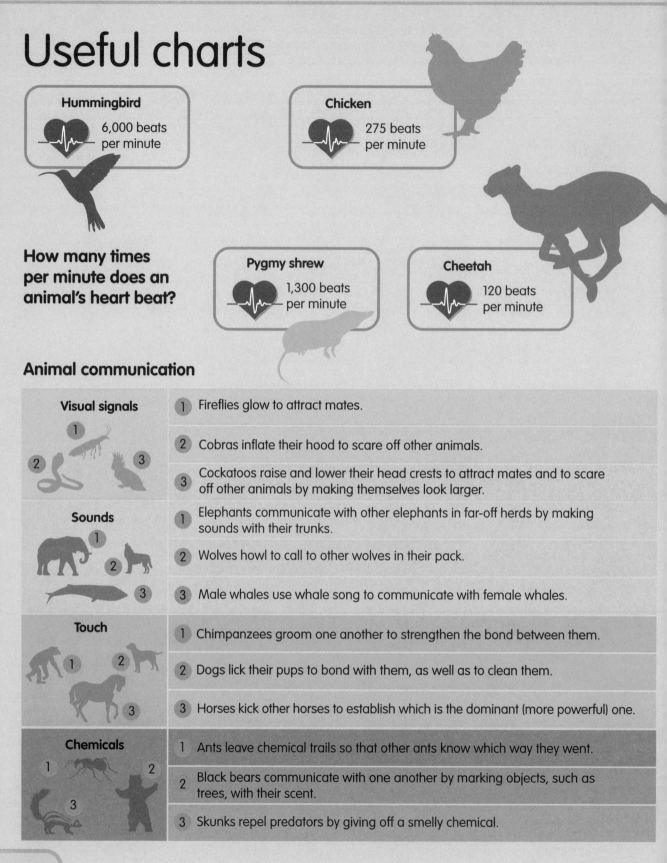

Hummingbird
6,000 beats per minute

Chicken
275 beats per minute

How many times per minute does an animal's heart beat?

Pygmy shrew
1,300 beats per minute

Cheetah
120 beats per minute

Animal communication

Visual signals		
	1	Fireflies glow to attract mates.
	2	Cobras inflate their hood to scare off other animals.
	3	Cockatoos raise and lower their head crests to attract mates and to scare off other animals by making themselves look larger.
Sounds	1	Elephants communicate with other elephants in far-off herds by making sounds with their trunks.
	2	Wolves howl to call to other wolves in their pack.
	3	Male whales use whale song to communicate with female whales.
Touch	1	Chimpanzees groom one another to strengthen the bond between them.
	2	Dogs lick their pups to bond with them, as well as to clean them.
	3	Horses kick other horses to establish which is the dominant (more powerful) one.
Chemicals	1	Ants leave chemical trails so that other ants know which way they went.
	2	Black bears communicate with one another by marking objects, such as trees, with their scent.
	3	Skunks repel predators by giving off a smelly chemical.

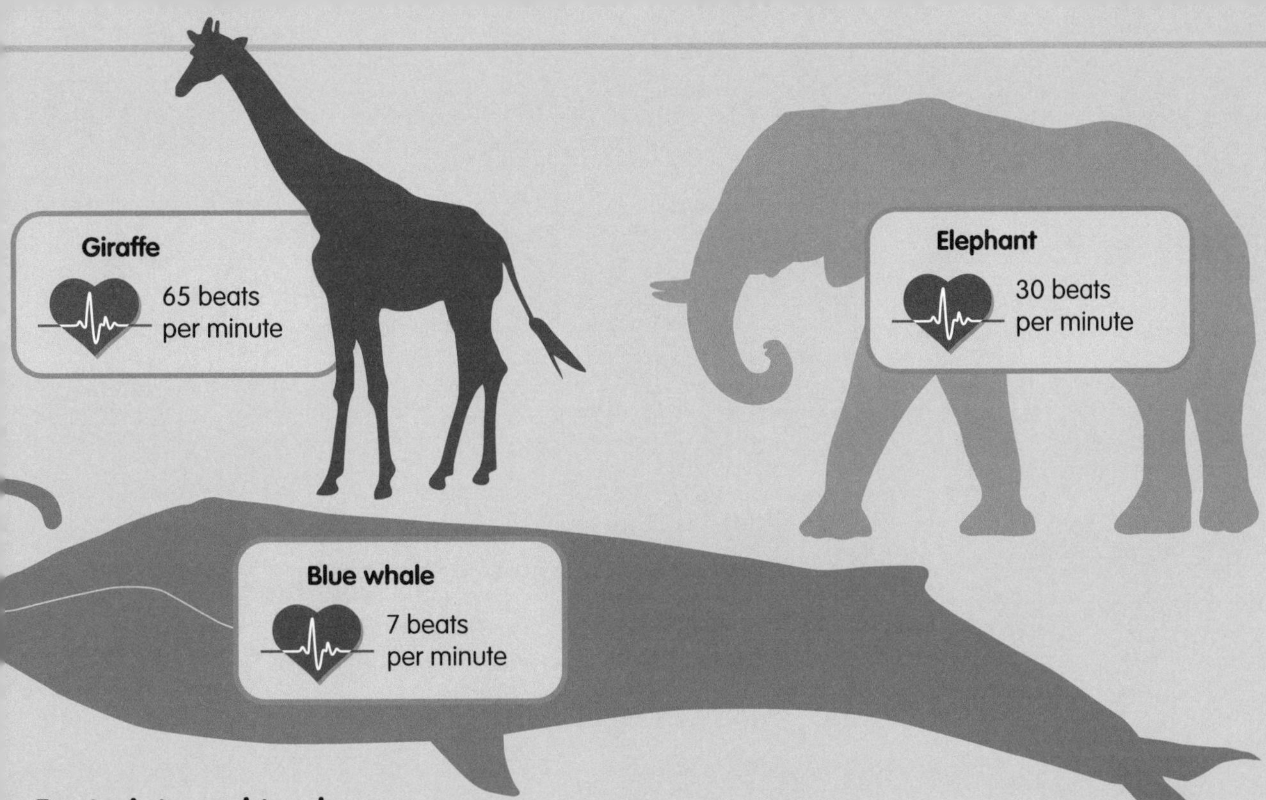

Giraffe

65 beats per minute

Elephant

30 beats per minute

Blue whale

7 beats per minute

Footprints and tracks

Animal	Animal shape	Footprints	Tracks
Weasel			
Turkey			
Fox			
Tiger			
Dog			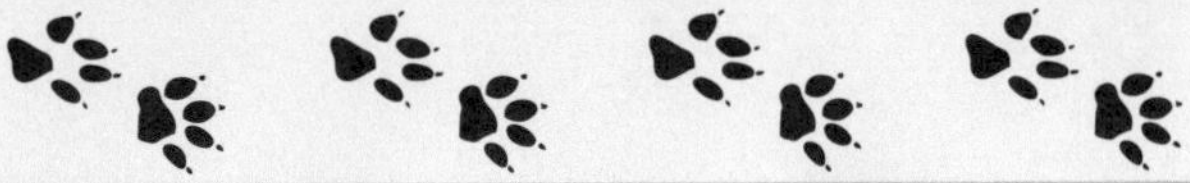
Deer			
Crow			

Glossary

adaptation
A special feature of a living thing that makes it better suited to its particular environment or way of life.

arachnid
An invertebrate with four pairs of legs.

arthropod
An invertebrate animal with jointed legs, a segmented body, and an exoskeleton.

brooding
When adult animals use their body to keep their eggs or young warm.

burrow
A hole or tunnel dug into the ground by an animal to create a home or a refuge from predators.

cartilage
A tough, flexible tissue found on the skeleton of vertebrates. The skeletons of sharks and rays are made entirely of cartilage.

courtship
The displays and behaviors that animals use to attract a mate.

crustacean
A group of arthropods that includes crabs and shrimp.

dormant
Describes a period during which an animal's normal physical functions slow down or stop working.

evolution
The process by which different kinds of living organisms have developed and diversified from earlier, often less complex life forms during the history of Earth.

exoskeleton
An external skeleton that supports and protects an animal's body. A crab's tough shell is its exoskeleton.

extinction
The permanent disappearance of a species.

gestation period
The period of development of an animal from the time it is conceived until its birth.

hibernation
When an animal spends the cold winter in a dormant state.

incubate
To hatch eggs by sitting on them and keeping them warm.

insect
A small arthropod with six legs and three body parts: head, thorax, and abdomen. Insects generally have two or four wings.

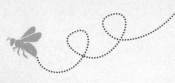

invertebrate
An animal without a backbone. About 95 percent of all animals are invertebrates.

life cycle
The pattern of changes that an animal undergoes as it develops over its lifetime.

life expectancy
The average period of time that an animal is expected to live.

marsupial
A mammal that develops inside its mother's pouch when it is a newborn.

mating
The coming together of a male and female animal during sexual reproduction.

molt
When an animal sheds its outer covering. Insects and crustaceans have to molt so that they can grow bigger.

parasite
A living thing that lives on or inside the body of another species of living thing, known as a host.

pheromone
A chemical emitted by an animal that has an effect on another member of the same species.

predator
An animal that kills and eats other animals.

prey
An animal that is hunted and killed by another animal for food.

regeneration
The regrowth of a body part, such as a leg or a tail.

reproduction
The production of offspring (young animals).

scales
Hard, overlapping plates that protect the skin of fish and reptiles.

species
A group of living organisms that contains individuals that can breed with one another.

streamlined
Describes an animal's body that is shaped to move through water or air easily.

venom
A poisonous fluid in an animal's bite or sting. Poison, by contrast, is swallowed or inhaled by the victim.

vertebrate
An animal with a backbone. There are five main types of vertebrates: mammals, birds, fish, reptiles, and amphibians.

Index

Find out more

📖 Books to read

Everything You Need to Know about Animals by Nicola Davies (Kingfisher, 2013)
Navigators: Animals by Miranda Smith (Kingfisher, 2012)
Encyclopedia of Animals by Karen McGhee and George McKay, PhD (National Geographic, 2009)
Usborne World of Animals by Susanna Davidson and Mike Unwin (Usborne, 2007)
DK Eyewitness Books Animal by Tom Jackson (DK, 2012)

Websites to visit

A website that catalogs animals from aardvarks to zebras:
http://animals.nationalgeographic.com/animals

Marvel at Australian marsupials:
www.australianwildlife.com.au/marsupials.htm

See animals pretending to be a different species—and discover why:
www.bbc.co.uk/nature/adaptations/Mimicry

Find out more about animals that develop in their mother's pouch:
www.sandiegozoo.org/animalbytes/t-marsupial.html

🏛 Places to visit

Meet different types of mammals in the Kenneth E. Behring Family Hall of Mammals,
part of the Smithsonian Institution National Museum of Natural History:
10th Street and Constitution Ave. NW, Washington, D.C. 20560
Phone: (202) 357-2700
www.mnh.si.edu/mammals

Dive into the world of aquatic animals at the Georgia Aquarium—
the largest aquarium in the world:
225 Baker Street NW, Atlanta, GA 30313
Phone: (404) 581-4000
www.georgiaaquarium.org

Interested to learn more about wild birds?
Take a flying visit to the World Bird Sanctuary:
125 Bald Eagle Ridge Road, Valley Park, MO 63088
Phone: (636) 225-4390, ext. 0
www.worldbirdsanctuary.org